A Stanislaw
Lem Reader

Rethinking Theory

General Editor
Gary Saul Morson

Consulting Editors
Robert Alter
Frederick Crews
John M. Ellis
Caryl Emerson

A Stanislaw Lem Reader

Peter Swirski

Northwestern University Press
Evanston, Illinois

Northwestern University Press
Evanston, Illinois 60208-4210

Compilation copyright © 1997 by Peter Swirski. "Thirty Years Later" by Stanislaw Lem translated from "Trzydzieści lat później," *Wiedza i Życie* (June 1991): 11–23; reprinted by permission of Stanislaw Lem. *A Stanislaw Lem Reader* published 1997 by Northwestern University Press.

Printed in the United States of America

ISBN 0-8101-1494-1 (cloth)
ISBN 0-8101-1495-X (paper)

Library of Congress Cataloging-in-Publication Data

A Stanislaw Lem reader / [edited by] Peter Swirski.
    p. cm. — (Rethinking theory)
    Includes bibliographical references.
    ISBN 0-8101-1494-1 (alk. paper). — ISBN 0-8101-1495-X (pbk. :
alk. paper)
    1. Lem, Stanisław—Interviews. 2. Authors, Polish—20th century—
Interviews. 3. Forecasting. 4. Literature and society. I. Lem,
Stanisław. II. Swirski, Peter. III. Series.
PG7158.L392A35   1997
891.8'537—dc21
                  97-23102
                  CIP

The paper used in this publication meets the minimum requirements of the American National Standard for Information Sciences—Permanence of Paper for Printed Library Materials, ANSI Z39.48-1984.

This book is dedicated to Stanislaw Lem and Paisley Livingston.

Contents

Stanislaw Lem: A Stranger in a Strange Land

A stranger in a strange land. Ever since Elizabeth Ashbridge coined this phrase to express her sense of alienation on arriving in America, it has become a standard metaphor for describing someone's sense of wonder and estrangement. These days the phrase appears equally frequently in works of fiction and of philosophy that target the future.

Robert Heinlein adopted this metaphor as the title of one his most popular novels about contact with the alien. Following H. G. Wells's (and especially Orson Welles's) *War of the Worlds,* contact with the alien conjures up images of extraterrestrial invasion, these days ossified into a tradition of low-budget, Ed Wood-type, Hollywood pictures. But things are not so simple in Heinlein's work. In *Stranger in a Strange Land* (1961), a messiah-like humanoid from Mars becomes a cult figure in circumstances which mock and satirize not so much the fundamentally not-so-strange stranger as the oddities of our own civilization. It is ourselves, examined through the distorting prism of Heinlein's narrative *Gedankenexperiment,* who emerge as the true strangers in a strange land of our alternative future.

To pack it with more resonance, the topos of a stranger in a strange land is often approached through a symmetrical inversion of its main elements. Thus an emissary from the Earth finds himself in the midst of an alien civilization, playing the unenviable role of a stranger in a strange land. Depending on the intentions of the writer, the reaction to the stranger's presence runs the gamut from xenophobic suspicion to veneration and reverence of the type usually reserved for beings of a higher order, like the demiurges or deities of antiquity.

The latter variant is exploited by the Russian writers, Arkady and Boris Strugatsky, in *Hard to Be a God* (1964). Rumata, an emissary from the Earth, is a deus ex machina witness to the feudal, fascist, and theocratic upheavals which tear the alien society apart. The Strugatskys' novel illustrates and evaluates several precise socio-historiographic theses, especially those with roots in turbulent twentieth-century Russian history. It scoffs at the messianic impatience of social revolutionaries for a "quick fix" to the agonizingly enduring socio-evolutionary problems of our times. The

Strugatskys caution that taking on responsibility for an alien race is as thankless a task as shaping the history and social development of our own.

The analogy between the foreign world of *Hard to Be a God* and our own is far from accidental. The strangeness is only an illusion; behind the alien society and its superficially unfamiliar names, places, or customs, there is always the sadly familiar Earth. It is no accident that the cognitive and emotional epiphany of estrangement is a paradigm of self-revelation. The envoy from our planet, striving to penetrate the veil of enigma and mystery which surrounds the alien race, finds himself in the position of the eponymous hero of Edgar Allan Poe's story "William Wilson." In a moment of terrible epiphany, when the protagonist tears the mask off the mysterious visitor, he sees only the contorted features so intimately familiar, because they are his own.

Although structurally antithetical, these two variants of estrangement meet on a deeper cognitive level, in both cases trying to tell us something significant about our own society. Both function by estranging the familiar and accentuating the relations that lie at the cultural center of today and tomorrow. In addition to the first two, there is one more fiction-specific version of the Brechtian *Verfremdungseffekt*. The third variant combines the first two, in order to alienate the reader from the contemporary world. The cognitive and emotional correlative is achieved by looking at ourselves from within our own culture. We need not automatically think at this point of the threadbare conventions of time travel. Far more striking and original is the stratagem employed by Poe in his less known "The Thousand-and-Second Tale of Scheherazade" (1845). In the story, instead of dispatching Sindbad to the future, the author sends him to the author's own mid nineteenth-century present, recounting Sindbad's amazement and incredulity at the natural and scientific wonders of Poe's contemporary world.

Notwithstanding Poe's remarkable narrative success in the middle of the nineteenth century, today, at the close of the twentieth, the reaction to this type of storytelling may understandably be more skeptical. Surely this type of estrangement could no longer work with the same efficacy in the present-day context. Novelty, surprise, and estrangement are a function of the absence of contextualizing information, but what could surprise us today, in the age in which, symbolically, Fort Knox has turned into a Data-Bank?

And yet, in a world where reality turns out so often to be stranger than fiction, where the accelerating pace of social events and scientific research makes one feel like a stranger in a strange land, the world of today seems more and more like a futuristic tale of tomorrow. How is that? Stellar probes are already on their way to other solar systems; the genetic code—though not yet the hereditary plasma—has already been altered in newborn babies; some forms of blindness can be remedied by plugging video terminals into sockets planted directly in the brain; the cloning of human embryos is now a fait accompli; infertile sixty-three-year-old women are now able to bear children; computer system and program aggregates—what the media are fond of calling "cyberspace"—are growing so rapidly in size and complexity that they may be on the verge of becoming nontransparent to human scrutiny; cyclotron-created antimatter, instead of annihilating on impact, can now be stored in "jars" made of magnetic fields; and so on and so forth.

The roster is practically endless, augmented daily with reports of events and phenomena which stun with their implications for our society and culture. Awe-inspiring as they are, however, the strange news is not from nowhere, but from the strange land of our own contemporary reality. If there is one thing it makes clear, it is that we are moving with escape velocity away from the familiar cultural equilibrium of yesterday, into the accelerating turmoil of tomorrow.

The structural order based on narrative estrangement gives striking and useful results when applied to the writings of Stanislaw Lem. Conventionally Lem's works have been chronologically divided into, roughly, the early phase of the 1950s, the "golden" period of the 1960s, the experimental stage of the 1970s, and the less known group of works—some still untranslated—from the 1980s.[1] The one immediate result of viewing Lem's literary career through the prism of estrangement is a perspective on his progressive refocusing from the themes of distant space and future to the present and pressing concerns of our society. From the perspective of four decades, his works display a clear shift from the cosmic theater of "there and then" to an intensifying preoccupation with the strangeness of the Earthly "here and now."

The earliest phase in Lem's writing illustrates well his cosmic search for enlightenment, with outer space serving as a backdrop to stories usually set in the faraway future. In the utopian future of *Astronauci* (*The Astronauts*, 1951), a spaceship is dispatched to Venus to explore an alien civilization, which, as the investigation reveals, perished accidentally while arming for a military invasion of Earth. *Obłok Magellana* (*The Magellan Nebula*, 1954) replicates this futuristic and expansive pattern but on a galactic scale. Gea, a planetoid-type spaceship from Earth, bears generations of human explorers in search of extraterrestrial life and intelligence. On a more satirical note, there is also *The Star Diaries*, a collection of short stories about the cosmic capers of Ijon Tichy, adventurer and homegrown philosopher par excellence, who roams the galaxy and records the strange familiarity of its peoples and cultures.

The second, "golden" phase in Lem's creativity, from which comes his most acclaimed novel, *Solaris*, adds a new dimension to this expansive, adventurous pattern aimed at the future and the cosmos. *Eden* (1959) depicts the peripeties of astronauts who, while investigating a strange planet, agonize over the same socio-evolutionary dilemmas that Rumata confronts in *Hard to Be a God*. *Solaris* (1961) begins to question the anthropomorphic premises behind the exploration of space. The protagonist, Chris Kelvin, is sent to a research station which is to monitor the behavior of a sentient "ocean" which covers the surface of the planet Solaris. To all appearances this is a routine mission; after long decades of research and exploration, Solaris is now considered a familiar, if still unexplained planet. Yet this time an unscheduled effort to establish contact with the ocean has profound consequences. Word turns into flesh when the ocean transforms memories extracted from the scientists' minds into living neutrino-based beings, driving humans to the brink of insanity. All thought of exploration is quickly forsaken in a frantic struggle to come to terms with the "invasion." Staggered by shock and doubt, the scientists concentrate instead on erasing every painful trace of the unwanted contact. Far from Earth, in the midst of the cosmic void, Kelvin and his colleagues finally glimpse the parabolic face of the universe—their own. A similar pattern is at work in another of Lem's novels from that period, *The Invincible* (1964). The work takes its title after a space cruiser dispatched to extend the military and scientific frontiers of Earth's future space civilization. Yet by the end of the novel, the Invincible and its crew are humbled and robbed of their anthropomorphic illusions in an encounter with a Black Cloud of strange microcrystals, a by-product of extraterrestrial cybernetic evolution.[2]

But even though this expansive, outwardly oriented pattern of narration is prominent in the first half of Lem's career, from the beginning we can discern a countertrend in his concerns. The virtually unknown *Człowiek z Marsa* (*Man from Mars*, 1946; which makes it de facto Lem's first published novel) has contemporary society as its focus, and displays few of the props associated with the exploration of space. Published only once as a serial in a Kraków magazine, *Man from Mars* censures the vicious tangle of military and political strategizing which turns the idea of cosmic contact into a farce, and ends in the cold-blooded destruction of the Martian visitor. This early work seems to presage Lem's eventual turn away from the epistemic concerns of the cosmic future and his return to the more immediate, if equally intractable, social and cultural dilemmas of our times.

This is not to say that *Man from Mars* is an isolated example even among Lem's early works. The thread of contemporary realism continues in *Szpital Przemienienia* (*Hospital of the Transfiguration*, 1955). The action of this novel takes place in a mental hospital during the first days of World War II.[3] The medical staff's moral and ethical dilemma between fleeing for safety before the invading Nazi troops, or staying to tend to the helpless patients, has lost nothing of its harrowing truth today, during the gory breakup of the Yugoslav federation. At the beginning of Lem's second phase we also find *The Investigation* (1959), a detective story contemporary (if not typical) in all respects. The novel describes a series of forensically and scientifically inexplicable "resurrections" from local morgues, which allows Lem to reflect on the explanatory nature and the epistemological a priori of Western philosophy.

Two years later appears *Memoirs Found in a Bathtub* (1961), another work which returns from the stars to focus on the socio-political insanity shaping Cold War reality. As in *Man from Mars,* this novel targets the social dangers implicated in and by military politics. Depicting the quixotic wanderings of a nameless espionage agent, Lem's *Memoirs*—in the tradition of the theater of the absurd, and with the blackest of humors—is a Kafkaesque correlative for the cultural void and the existential post-traumatic stress disorder which make the latter half of the twentieth century such a confused and chaotic time.[4]

Lem's drive toward greater realism and immediacy of social concerns from that period is documented in a series of nonfictional monographs. Although not available in English, they are legendary from the accounts of those able to read them in their native Polish, or in the Russian or German translations. *Dialogi* (*Dialogues*, 1957) is a record of Lem's analysis of the then still novel field of cybernetics, externalized by means of Berkeleyan dialogues between Philonous and Hylas. Written from the perspective of a social scientist, the book marks Lem's growing involvement in the reality of his social present. In the first, theoretical part the author recapitulates the fundamental concepts and accomplishments of the new science. In the second he launches an applied cybernetic analysis and critique of the main political and economic formations known from modern history. The objectivity, acumen, and integrity of Lem's analyses guarantee that they never turn into a diatribe against any specific ideological or politico-economic system. Even more important, his hypotheses and diagnoses have lost nothing of their pertinence today, forty years after they were first written.

Lem's nonfictional ambitions are even more apparent in his most extensive philosophical work to date, *Summa technologiae* (1964). *Summa* is a landmark work of futurology in which Lem attempts to chart out the future course of our civilization's pan-instrumental development. As the author puts it, *Summa* is a "cybernetic interpretation of the past and future of Man . . . a picture of the Cosmos seen with the eyes of the Constructor . . . a study of the engineering of the powers of Nature and of human hands . . . a collection of hypotheses too bold to claim scientific accuracy" (5). Picking up the thread of the fictions from the same period, but turning his attention toward home, Lem develops a series of wide-ranging prognoses on the social, cultural, and technological destiny of our civilization. Virtual reality, information "breeding," cosmic expansion, or teleporting are just a few hypotheses with which Lem bridges the discussion of the technology of today with supertechnology of the future.

Still, during the academic debates which followed the publication of his futurological masterpiece, Lem distanced himself from an uncritical faith in humanity's cognitive development. Instead he would point with dismay to our ubiquitous and seemingly unstoppable drive for conflict and aggression. This was in itself a significant change in a writer who, up to this point, still subscribed to Enlightenment ideals, according to which humanity could transcend tribalism and build a better future on a planetary scale. With hindsight, however, it is Lem's vintage *Man from Mars*, with its stark images of mistrust and aggression, which captures the bitter and almost accusatory tone nurtured in his later, more mature novels.

The quintessential fiction of this period, which culminates the second and most prolific phase in Lem's career, is *His Master's Voice* from 1968. It may be somewhat misleading to classify this work as a novel, overshadowed as it is by the tone and format of a philosophical essay and a spiritual diary. A coded neutrino message from outer space is the narrative and philosophical catalyst with which Lem estranges the reader from concerns which otherwise would have been only too familiar: military takeover of scientific research, nuclear superpower rivalry with its narrow-minded chauvinism, excess pride and lack of humility of the political and military establishment, and humanity's perennial capacity for (self-)destruction.

His Master's Voice marks Lem's return from the stars for good. With only minor exceptions, the twin problems of contemporary, or currently anticipated, cultural developments dominate his writing to this very day. This trend is reflected and, if anything, intensified in his nonfiction of that period. In 1968, that is, at the same time as *His Master's Voice,* Lem published his extensive study of literary culture, theory, and scholarship entitled *Filozofia przypadku* (*The Philosophy of Chance*). In it he applied himself to the other of C. P. Snow's "Two Cultures," theorizing on the subjects of culture, art, literature, literary scholarship, criticism, aesthetics, and axiology (among others).[5]

The year 1970 saw the publication of an equally ambitious and extensive two-volume monograph devoted to—in Lem's view—the related disciplines of futurology and science fiction. In this encyclopedic study, the author traces the cognitive parallels, aesthetic differences, and shared social responsibilities of the science of futurology and the literary genre of science fiction. *Fantastyka i futurologia* (*Science Fiction and Futurology*) again sets Lem as a stranger in the strange land of poststructuralist excesses. Lem's departure from its canons is unmistakable. His strangeness is that of an epistemic realist and antirelativist, a proponent of forging cognitive connections between the assembly of aesthetic artifacts known as literature and their social context, without reducing either to a well-known canon of academic "isms."

Lem's critical analysis of the sociology and structuralist aesthetics of science fiction are especially accurate, and his commentary on the genre's past and present ghetto status have lost nothing of their accuracy during the intervening years. Today, much as when *Science Fiction and Futurology* was first published, any bookstore provides ample evidence as to how far science fiction has (d)evolved from its brave new origins. This stimulating literary form which, in Europe, boasts H. G. Wells, Karel Čapek, and Olaf Stapledon among its progenitors, has been relegated to that neutered marketing hybrid of sci-fi/fantasy. The economic pressures of the marketplace reflect, and are in turn reflected, in the amorphousness of the genre, whose cognitive and literary ambitions are symbolized by its lurid covers, full of advertising clichés.

Yet sporadically one may still find, amid the broadsword-wielding, time-jumping, cyberspace-hacking average, works of great originality and erudition. These artistically and philosophically ambitious novels are true strangers in the strange land of a Star Trek aficionado, and some of the most challenging (and experimental) among them were written by Stanislaw Lem in the 1970s and early 1980s. This third phase in Lem's writing includes a collection of metaliterary experiments published as *A Perfect Vacuum* (1971); *Imaginary Magnitude* (1973) and *Golem XIV* (1981; included in the English edition of *Imaginary Magnitude*); and the genre-defying short novels, *The Futurological Congress* (1971) and *Chain of Chance* (1976).

The format which Lem employs with such success in *A Perfect Vacuum* is a review of unwritten and nonexistent works, including a bravado tongue-in-cheek review by Lem the critic of *A Perfect Vacuum* by Lem the writer. This ironic collection, reviewing an entire array of fictive novels, exposes what Lem sees as the dead ends of contemporary culture. He denounces its value systems and especially its overintellectualized self-centeredness which, notwithstanding a chorus of laudations from the critics, is impotent before the profundity of contemporary social and cultural problems. Lem goes so far as to argue that art itself has failed in its historical role as an emotional and philosophical registrar of culture and society. The art world, flooded by mass produced genre clones, is no longer capable of bringing the contemporary world to justice in a Poe-like moment of terrible but illuminating epiphany.

The problems which Lem dissects in *A Perfect Vacuum* are of immediate concern not only to literary critics and theoreticians. One of his central arguments—to which he returns with almost manic intensity—is that the fashionable poststructuralist experiments in literature, combined with the complacent response from cultural curators, have precipitated its almost total infertility. Lem argues that one of the main reasons for this flight of art from reality is a complete leveling out of cultural (including literary-critical) evaluative efforts. This process is, in turn, feedback-linked to inflationary trends characterizing contemporary publishing and advertising practices, which the author mercilessly targets in *A Perfect Vacuum*.

"Pericalypsis," for example, could have been written only in the twentieth century, the age of information explosion, with the specter of unknown Shakespeares buried under mountains of print. Lem's story identifies the need for some sort of capping process to the continuous outpouring of printed words. However, one is compelled to ask, how is such filtering of published material to be effected? In game theoretic terms there is a minimum payoff—the act of publication—that each and every writer/player can get individually. The optimum strategy for individuals outside a coalition is to make moves which guarantee them the minimum payoff. And, despite Lem's prototypic "Save the Human Race Foundation," proposed tongue-in-cheek in "Pericalypsis," there is little hope of successfully forming a coalition which will pay artists *not* to create. This situation would resemble too vividly one of the absurdities in *Catch-22*, where the more alfalfa farmers do not produce, the more they get paid for not producing it.

Where *A Perfect Vacuum* addresses itself to art and literature, *Imaginary Magnitude* is more anthropological and sociological in its impetus. This time Lem has written an eclectic collection of prefaces, forewords, and introductions to unwritten books which, according to him, should nevertheless exist. In the collection he parodies some of the naive but popular futurological scenarios, while hypothesizing on ideas whose extravagance extends beyond the scope of contemporary scientific theories.

In *Golem XIV*, Lem's farthest-reaching attempt to stake out the conceptual limits of humanity's future, the author engages in futuristic prognostication of the anticipated progress in the cognitive and bio-sciences. Using as his narrative alter ego an eighteenth-binasty (*bitic dynasty*) computer prodigy, Lem contends that the revolutionary advancement in the sciences will usurp the conceptual ground traditionally claimed by philosophy (whether ethics, epistemology, aesthetics, or metaphysics) and even religion. He also calls into question our ability to control and utilize this process for the greater benefit of all people. The bleak, detached, almost clinically analytic tone of Lem's discussion underlies his growing skepticism as to the rationality of *Homo sapiens*, whom—just like Jonathan Swift before him—he sees merely as *Homo rationis capax*.

After devoting the first part of his career to the exploration of humanity's place in the cosmos, from the mid-1960s onward Lem has applied himself with increasing urgency to the task of defining and interpreting humanity's place on Earth. During the 1980s the urgency not only has not abated but has assumed critical proportions, felt especially in his latest (and probably last) novel, *Fiasco* (1987). This farewell work is a fit conclusion to Lem's career as a fiction writer, in which the parabolic depiction of the planet Quinta allows him to express his concern for the future of Earth. The novel openly alludes to many leitmotifs from his earlier works, even to the point of symbolically resurrecting Pirx, the eponymous protagonist of the popular *Tales of Pirx the Pilot* (1959–68) and *More Tales of Pirx the Pilot* (1965–83).

Fiasco illustrates how, under the pressure of shortsighted and pragmatist realpolitik, ethical and moral edicts can be subverted to justify social and military oppression. Stunned by our potential for succumbing to the madness of strategic violence, Lem contemplates the scarcity of chances for survival of the human species, using the death of an alien race to illustrate the (self-)destructive tendencies of our civilization. It is no accident that Quinta, to which the Earthmen trek across the stars, ends up massacred by the arsenals wielded by Earth scientists who, despite their edifying efforts to maintain professional neutrality, succumb to the paranoia of local power struggles. Lem, the impassioned rationalist, concludes from the human experience on Earth that a chance disturbance in any such fragile equilibrium (on Quinta represented by the arrival of humans) can lead to its collapse and the potential destruction of the planetary civilization, whether Quintan or our own.

Fiasco gives voice to our contemporary anxieties not in terms of abstract ontological, moral, and ethical axioms, but by relating them to the immediate reality of the social and political present. With constant references to military technology, its destructive potential, its calculated strategy—so many that they threaten to overwhelm the second half of the novel—Lem warns of the incessant threat of the armament race which, despite a proliferation of treaties and an end to the Cold War, shows few signs of dissipating.

Until now a patient, if acerbic, observer and moralist, Lem predicts in all earnestness that our species might be on the way to imminent destruction. If we juxtapose this view with the hopes still expressed in the mid-1960s in *The Invincible*—that humanity will balance the exploration of the universe at all costs with the recognition of the inevitable limitations of anthropocentrism—the result is a picture of a writer who has comprehended the limits of his humanism. How can we seek contact with other civilizations if we continue to wage war with fellow members of our own species? How are we to achieve understanding with aliens when we cannot accomplish the same here on Earth?

The period between *Golem* in 1981 and *Fiasco* in 1987, which Lem spent largely abroad following the imposition of martial law in Poland, was very productive. It saw the publication of *Wizja lokalna* (*On Site Inspection,* 1983), *Prowokacja* (*Provocation,* 1984), *Biblioteka XXI wieku* (in English as *One Human Minute,* 1986), and *Pokoj na ziemi* (*Peace on Earth,* 1987). All these works are full of bitter and ironic reflections on the future of our society and of Lem's growing condemnation of the socio-political practices of our times.

On Site Inspection contains a tragic vision of a technologically splendid society which surrenders its own freedom to intellectronic nanomachines in order to put an end to the menace that it harbors within itself. The wide-ranging measures of social order and security on the alien planet recall the "soft" totalitarianism of *Return from the Stars* (1961), even though for the first time Lem seems to consider the suppression of one's individuality a lesser evil than the perennial and all-too-real drive to aggression. The beast within, which was previously confined to the range of primitive clubs, slings, spears, or arrows, can now be released to sow death on the planetary—or, as *Fiasco* illustrates, even interplanetary—scale.

The subject of death is nothing new in Lem's work. One only needs to recall the Nazi invasion in *Time Not Lost,* the self-destruction of the Venusian civilization in *The Astronauts,* the concentration camps of *Eden,* the cybernetic "necrosphere" of *The Invincible,* the macrotunneling effect which almost becomes the ultimate mass weapon in *His Master's Voice,* the starving and dying humanity drugged into beatific stupor in *The Futurological Congress,* or the "necrobiosis" of a culture which has instrumentally realized the dream of immortality in *On Site Inspection.* Not surprisingly, then, the subject is picked up again in Lem's next major work from the 1980s, *Provocation.*

In the Polish edition this book/essay is made up of two reviews of two fictive (nonexistent) works of nonfiction: *Der Völkermord* by Horst Aspernicus, and *One Human Minute* by J. and S. Johnson. Through his review of the fictive Aspernicus's work, Lem conducts a broad cultural analysis of the role of death in modern desacralized society. As his analytic base he uses the factual material of the genocide perpetrated by the Nazis in the occupied territories during World War II. At the same time he tries to account for the morbid ubiquity of death—especially in its most violent incarnations, such as terrorism—in contemporary society. In an attempt to reintegrate the Nazi atrocities into the order of the Mediterranean civilization, Lem accuses modern culture of denying death the cultural prominence which it has hitherto enjoyed due to the previously unchallenged status of its Judeo-Christian roots.

In the course of his discussion, Lem proposes explicit historiosophic and anthropological theses regarding the symbolic and institutional functioning of death in the context of its modern reutilization. Specifically, he maintains that the patchwork synthesis of the ethics of evil and aesthetics of kitsch—which gave rise to the mass murders of the German extermination juggernaut—returns in a modified, fragmented form in today's cultural reality. As an example Lem points to state and antistate terrorism, ritualized violence in art and the media, political extremism, the ultra-right turn to neofascism in electoral practice, and the lasting attraction of death as an ultimate cultural bastion to be defeated.

Any social formation that denounces the cultural significance of death by relegating it to a barely tolerated necessity fails to realize that, sooner or later, in one form or another, the banished issue is bound to return. Once we accept, however, that there is no escape from the dictates of our biological selves, it is easier to see that almost all cultural and life choices derive their sense and essence from our mortality. The striving for progress or achievement, the instinct for procreation or fame, all derive their rationale and raison d'être from the ineradicable presence of death. Attempts to sweep the subject of death under the carpet of the group subconscious lead only to suicide or genocide, sanctioned by the dictates of one ideology or another.

It was the cultural domestication of death, combined with the inversion (or rather perversion) of its symbolic and real value, that enabled Nazi

Germany to justify its eugenic Aryan ideology, together with acts of mass slaughter and genocide. Lem's fictional review of a nonexistent socio-anthropological study—one which, in his opinion, clearly ought to exist—documents the presence of a vast cultural domain all too often neglected by contemporary sociologists, historians, and cultural philosophers.

There is an almost anecdotal incident that illustrates once again the extent to which Lem's writings at this later stage blur the line between fiction and nonfiction, between imaginary events and imaginative renditions of real ones, between the cognitive impulses behind fictive and factual writing. In a 1984 interview with Peter Engel, Lem describes a whimsical encounter between an acquaintance of his—a professor of contemporary history—and a member of the Polish Academy of Science. The meeting took place in Berlin, shortly after the publication of *Provocation*, which apparently made quite an impression on the member of the academy. During the conversation, the historian remarked to him, "I believe that Lem wrote a review of that book," to which the other replied, "I don't know if Lem wrote anything, but I've got the book at home!" (230). One can only wonder about the power of a fictional review which impresses readers to such an extent that they imagine its imaginary subject *must* exist—more, that they own the book in question . . .

For years Lem's works, couched in the guise of fictive metacommentaries, imaginary publications, allegorical or philosophical fables, or even outright speculative treatises, have departed from mainstream fiction writing. It was thus an interesting move for a writer who had often complained of being tired of conventional fabulation, to return to it in a couple of pivotal Ijon Tichy novels: *On Site Inspection* (1983) and *Peace on Earth* (1987). Through their protagonist, both hark back to the earlier cycle of Tichy short stories: the regularly expanded *Star Diaries* (first edition 1957; in English also *Memoirs of a Space Traveler,* 1981), which, despite the hilarity of the hero's (mis)adventures, always contains a serious didactic strain.

In *Peace on Earth,* in order to free our planet from the threat of mass destruction, all national arsenals are transferred to the moon. The satellite becomes a massive international armory of future weapons systems de-signed on the principle of natural biological evolution (they can multiply and mutate using the sun for energy and the lunar soil for raw materi-als). The novel opens at the point when miscellaneous lobbying groups blackmail the UN into action with threats that the military equilibrium on the moon has been breached, creating a new and unknown generation of weapons which could eventually turn against the Earth. It is decided that an impartial human observer should be sent to the moon, and the honor is bestowed on Tichy.

The outcome of Tichy's mission (itself related in a series of flashbacks) surpasses all misgivings. The moon's ecological environment has been taken over by micropolymers—a kind of intellectronic pollen, capable of transforming into symbiotic bacterialike species. These "necrocytes" give life to "selenocytes" which, being even more versatile, wipe out the older generations of weapons systems. At the first opportunity, the selenocytes invade the Earth by way of Tichy's spaceship and then, assuming the form of computer viruses, attack all computer systems and their programs. In the pan-computerized twenty-first century, it takes only a single day for the human race, deprived of its infrastructure, industrial base, and telecommunications, to be pushed to the brink of calamity reminiscent of the "papyralysis" and the collapse of human civilization in *Memoirs Found in a Bathtub*.

The evolution of inanimate matter is one of the perennial topics in Lem's philosophical investigations. The birth and evolution of "miniaturobots" was discussed already in *Summa technologiae* and found a narrative expression in the form of the Black Cloud of miniaturized crystals in *The Invincible*. The idea of organisms that lack intelligence and react only instinctively to signs of immediate danger returns in "The Upside Down Evolution" (in *One Human Minute*, 1986). In this story/essay, mass production of "synsect" weapon systems marks a qualitatively new stage in the history of human warfare. Where previously the conventionality of war arsenals entailed the conventionality of declaring and conducting hostilities, in the anarchic future painted by Lem, hostile actions of independent and autonomous synsects are indistinguishable from natural disasters occasionally ravaging the Earth (diseases, acid rain, landslides, earthquakes, etc.). The difference between war and peace is obliterated and replaced by a much more horrific era of crypto-hostilities, where all sides participate in the secret use of weapons so secret that not even their creators can tell them from phenomena of nature.

But the astuteness of Lem's prognoses on the subject of future technology, whether military or any other, is not the only factor which contributes to the overall value of his works. Although Lem's fictions are always formidable instruments of cognition, they are more than mere fictional illustrations of scientific and epistemological dilemmas. Their value owes as much to their artistic and aesthetic qualities as to their success in defining the forefront of our technology-driven culture. Perhaps the most powerful among those qualities is Lem's haunting symbolism, frequently touched by sadness and tragedy.

One unforgettable example is the dementia experienced by Tichy in *Peace on Earth*. During the lunar mission, without the protagonist's knowledge or consent, he is subjected to a procedure which truncates the nerve links between his brain hemispheres. Tichy's futile efforts to come to terms with his new and alien psycho-physical identity is an emblem of the agony of a contemporary Everyman. The protagonist's struggles with his subconscious and his altered patterns of behavior are a symbol of our times—a metaphor for the trauma that the human psyche has sustained in confrontation with the alienating bestiality of the twentieth century. The inner tortures experienced by Tichy, his efforts to find some modus vivendi, symbolize humanity's efforts to reconsolidate the shattered universe in a search for some values around which the fragmented culture can rally.

This, in brief outline, is the portrait of Stanislaw Lem as a stranger in a strange land. Still, it might appear contentious, perhaps even iconoclastic, to pin the label of "stranger" on a writer who has certainly had his share of recognition and success. Called a cultural movement unto himself, hailed as a grand master of European letters, Lem has been featured many times in the Nobel Prize shortlist for his country. His works have enjoyed a staggering number of translations into almost forty languages, as well as almost unbelievable publishing figures, approaching twenty five million worldwide.

During his career he has been the recipient of myriad literary awards; he has been an eagerly consulted philosopher, futurologist, theorist, reviewer, and critic. His reputation has crossed the boundaries of the literary world, with more and more commentators showing interest in his contribution to philosophy and philosophy of science. In a class by himself, stubbornly following the call of his difficult muse, Lem is indeed a strange phenomenon: a writer of fiction, who commands attention and respect from scientists, philosophers, critics, scholars, and writers—from John Updike to Kurt Vonnegut to Anthony Burgess—alike.

Whence the strangeness, then? A partial answer is suggested by Michael Kandel in his "Lem in Review (June 2238)." As Kandel describes it, Lem's scientific and philosophical pansophism is staggering in its proportions. It encompasses cybernetics, information theory, probability, game theory, linguistics, theory of automata, computing, genetics, biology, cosmology, ethics, anthropology, sociology, aesthetics, and literary studies, to name just a few. But the differences between Lem and his literary contemporaries are more profound, owing not so much to his encyclopedic knowledge or almost unbelievable range of interests as to his attitude toward knowledge and cognition.

I have remarked elsewhere that, rather than treating Lem's writings as individual opera, we should see them as a single monumental opus, consisting of so many chapters (represented by individual works), which can be ordered and reordered to yield new insights into his works and into the problems they touch on.[6] If there is a single overarching theme in this kaleidoscope of novels, stories, monographs, essays, studies, reviews, critiques, futurological predictions, philosophical speculations, and literary experiments, it is Lem's uncompromising view of literature's role in the contemporary cultural environment. His views on literary realism reveal that the many narrative conventions circulating in the literary world are of little use to him. For Lem realism is literature's way of confronting real and pressing problems which have already come, or are in the process of coming into existence, or those that will lie on the path of humanity's tomorrow. In fact, he concedes that this type of realism could be described simply as "sound prognosticating."[7]

In the final analysis, this is probably the most profound sense in which Lem is a stranger in a strange land. In a day when the humanistic part of our culture, and especially its academic element, persistently questions the objectivity and even rationality of epistemic criteria, Lem's philosophical and literary work is a strong voice to the contrary. In his writings, which constantly redefine and reinvent the concept of "literature," Lem plots the course for tomorrow with the imperfect knowledge of today. In his hands literature is a modeling vehicle, a flexible medium for developing socio-cultural hypotheses, an instrument of cognition and intellectual exploration, and a humanist avant-garde of contemporary culture.

From the perspective of forty years we can see that, far from escaping into outer space, Lem's works blend into a single *magnum opus* with Earth and its future as its twin foci. In fact, in view of the universality of this theme, I would argue that almost all of Lem's works are a source of fictional and nonfictional models for a single historiosophic scenario. His novels, stories, and essays model plausible socio-cultural reactions to powerful new stimuli, often of global proportions. Inventing fictional crises to portray the flexibility of our culture's potential response, Lem suggests—correctly in my opinion—that the stable (dynamic) equilibrium of a sufficiently large cultural system will tend to dominate its overall pattern of behavior.

The easiest way to illustrate the principle of dynamic equilibrium is to consider a simple closed system consisting of a bowl and a ball. Its initial equilibrium state is when the ball rests on the bottom of the bowl. The system is stable since occasional perturbations fail to prevent its return to the original equilibrium state. Every time an outside force of a finite nature (e.g., a human hand) rolls the ball up the side of the bowl, on withdrawal of the force the ball will return to its most probable state, coming to rest on the bottom again. The system will behave in the described manner only until the point where the ball is balanced on the rim in perfect symmetry. As this unstable kind of symmetry will inevitably be broken, the ball will roll either into or out of the bowl. In the latter case, it will again reach an equilibrium, but only as part of a completely new configuration (the same effect can be achieved by increasing the force violently enough to send the ball flying out and away from the bowl).

All futurological writing, so popular especially since becoming a well-paid industry in the 1960s and 1970s (under the aegis of, among others, the Club of Rome and the Rand Corporation), focuses primarily on the change aspect of the future. How the future will differ from today is the ruling and, surprisingly often, the only parameter in any scenario forecast. Little consideration is given to the possibility that, almost paradoxically, the challenges of tomorrow might turn out to be not so different from the challenges of today. In the French language this phenomenon is expressed as *plus ça change, plus c'est la même chose;* in fiction it is known as the Rip van Winkle syndrome, an enduring story of timelessness that defies a superficial facelift.

Lem's works flesh out the psycho-social consequences of this thesis in a variety of narrative and futurological scenarios. Formulating fictional models for what might be dubbed a Law of Preservation of Cultural Momentum, Lem debunks the fantasy of social enlightenment programs, whereby

radically new social forces—wars, revolutions, scientific discoveries—
might produce utopian peace and prosperity on Earth. Are we ready to
accept Lem's hypotheses? If so, we might have to admit that our problems
and conflicts are of our own design and that, as such, they are here to stay;
that small incremental improvements are all we can hope for from even
the most dramatic revolutions; that our cultural policies might have more
lasting and wide-ranging effects than we often suspect when implementing
them; that culture does abhor a vacuum; and that the sooner we come to
terms with these insights, the better for us and our future.

The evolutionary momentum of our culture gives it a tendency to adopt
and adapt to changing circumstances, rather than to collapse in their face.
On the other hand, its ability to adapt (plasticity) is clearly not infinite,
and can, under special conditions, be exceeded. Cultural plasticity will
accommodate centrifugal pressures only to a certain degree, after which
the culture will either dissolve entirely or, more likely, establish a radically
new form of equilibrium (like the ball in our example, which might now
come to rest in the corner of the room).

Even if any single factor may not affect culture to a catastrophic degree,
the combined effect of several destabilizing factors might. Today it is
becoming increasingly obvious that we do not have to look to outer space
for such a synergistic combination. Gene doctoring, population explosion,
nearsighted fiscal policies, eco-damage, new reproduction technologies,
breakdown of families, rise of ultranationalism, the information highway,
"smart" weapons, tactical nukes—the list is endless. It is impossible to
predict whether the fusion of these and other factors will destabilize
our culture to the point where it will cave in, perhaps to reassemble in
completely novel and unpredictable ways. We must not, however, stop
examining these factors for any signs of the jolt which might send us, so
to speak, out of our cultural bowl.

Experience and hindsight teach that, in one way or another, all these
new trends and phenomena will probably be assimilated into an everyday
part of our lives. The same experience and hindsight also teach that this
process usually happens without any deliberate plan of action on anybody's
part. In fact, the usual response to cultural revolutions is usually of the
"too little, too late" variety. As a result, the full potential of such cultural
revolutions, novel technologies, legal and ethical precedents, and the like is
never realized. Nor are we always better off for having them in the first place.

And this is precisely where mature literature can make a contribution—plotting the likely social consequences of such cultural transformations and developing anthropo-historical theses regarding psycho-social responses to new technologies. Such an ambitious agenda forms, of course, an equal challenge to the producers and consumers of fiction. In the end, it is no coincidence that Lem makes such great demands not only on himself but on his readers as well. For if we look closely at his lifelong creative metaphor, even though his vehicle is frequently a futurological scenario, his tenor is always a variation on an Earthly theme.[8]

Peter Swirski, Concordia University

Notes

1. In 1995 Harcourt published two new releases: *Highcastle* and *Peace on Earth.*

2. See my "Of Games with the Universe: Preconceptions of Science in Stanislaw Lem's *The Invincible.*"

3. This novel was actually completed in September 1948, i.e., before the publication of *The Astronauts,* which is usually listed as Lem's first work. Due to the complexities of the political and publishing situation during the Stalinist 1940s, *Hospital of the Transfiguration* was not published until 1955, and then only as part of the trilogy *Time Not Lost.* After 1975 Lem allowed to reprint only the first book, the earliest and independently written *Hospital.*

4. For an extensive analysis of this novel, see my "Game Theory in the Third Pentagon: A Study in Strategy and Rationality."

5. C. P. Snow, *The Two Cultures and a Second Look* (Cambridge: Cambridge University Press, [1959] 1964).

6. See my "A Literary Monument Revisited," 416.

7. Istvan Csicsery-Ronay, Jr., "Twenty-Two Answers and Two Postscripts: An Interview with Stanislaw Lem," 244.

8. I want to thank Ellen R. Feldman and the editorial staff at Northwestern University Press for their help in preparing this book for publication.

Reflections on Literature, Philosophy, and Science
(Personal Interview with Stanislaw Lem, June 1992)

Peter Swirski: *It is frequently proposed that literature should be an imaginative and cognitive forefront of our increasingly technology-driven society and culture. On the other hand we can observe the retreat of fiction from a sustained, coherent engagement of cognitive issues, and an escape into the never-never land of fantasy, magic, or ritualized genre games. Do you think that literary fiction can, or should, play a significant philosophical, and perhaps even prognostic, role in our society? Or are we asking it to perform tasks which might be incompatible with its aesthetic and artistic goals?*

Stanislaw Lem: Let me approach this question through an example taken from Kafka. From the artistic point of view there is no special difference between *The Castle* and "Penal Colony." On the other hand, the latter work seems to anticipate in some nightmarish way the concentration camps of the Third Reich, which in Kafka's times obviously did not yet exist. Yet this prognostic value is not usually perceived as an immanent component of Kafka's writing, simply because we are not used to—and do not have the analytic means for—approaching works of literature from the point of their prognostic correctness.

Take another sterling example, Huxley's *Brave New World*. It is simply not true that we approach and appreciate this work from the standpoint of whether his Alphas, Betas, and Gammas are really a part of our reality, that is, whether in the meantime they have come true. This novel, today already a little dated and old-fashioned, was rightly esteemed in its time, but not because people thought that it depicted the world exactly the way it would turn out to be. It is significant that even when prognostic literature teaches readers to recognize or even detect certain phenomena, whether social or any other, or when a work of fiction indeed presciently anticipates future trends, this does not yet automatically increase its literary value. This is one side of the issue—the prognostic merit in fiction.

On the other hand, we have the problem of the cognitive value of fiction, which requires a slightly different approach. What we are talking about here is the construction of models, most commonly of sociological nature, but not only—an undertaking which I sometimes refer to as "plying the sociological imagination." I must admit that the appalling paucity in this domain is the single element which I have always found the most dissatisfying in all fiction. Anyway, when speaking of the cognitive value of literature, we must acknowledge the presence of a periphrastic, or allegoric-periphrastic approach often taken by writers of fiction.

A good illustration of this type of narrative strategy can by found in the work of the Strugatsky brothers, Boris and Arkady. Most of their fictions are savage caricatures of Soviet totalitarianism and its internal relations. They protest that no one can be made happy by force, denounce the massive abuses within the system, and so forth. Their *Hard to Be a God* is possibly the best example of this type of writing. It is hardly surprising then, that from the moment when the Soviet system fell apart, one can see a curious and symptomatic development in the Strugatskys' works. In the past they used to skirt as closely as possible—keeping in mind the practices of Soviet censorship—the admissible limits of belletristic creativity. In their case they had to camouflage their social and political opposition to the regime. Naturally, when this facet of their writing was recognized by the Soviet critics at some point during the 1960s, various informants and delators—in their capacity as literary critics, of course—inflicted a lot of harm on these writers (keeping their works from being printed, etc.).

It is characteristic that this type of literature, which refers only to a very concrete type of totalitarian relations, loses a lot of its social relevance and vitality when the system which it critiques collapses. When the system lies in ruins, it turns out that there is no need to speak in Aesop's language, no need for complex periphrases and allusions, since now everything can be said simply as is. That is the reason why some writers lose the battle for cultural and artistic survival: history consigns to the garbage bin, as the Marxists used to say, the very thing they had tried to undermine and deride.

Recently I had a chance to discuss my own *Memoirs Found in a Bathtub* with a literary critic from Argentina. This meeting and the way he inter-preted what happens in my novel were for me a source of an important revelation. You know *Memoirs*: everyone spies on everyone else, the concept of espionage is elevated to an absolute and ultimate order, with spies sub-verted by the other side and vice versa, to the point where nobody knows any longer who is working for whom, including the spies themselves. This critic told me point blank: "You've described Argentina."

It turns out that my work was for him a perfect model of the Argentinean dictatorship. Clearly, it was of no consequence to him that I have never even been to South America. On the other hand, if you consider the insidious structure of ubiquitous suspicion which I described in *Memoirs*—the multiple masks which the agents wear so that no one can see their real faces—it is clear that all this refers to much more than just a single socio-political formation. Thus even when a given socio-political formation falls apart, a work of literature can retain its autonomy owing to the fact that it models universal phenomena that express certain regularities of social nature.

I must confess that I am not a writer oriented par excellence politically; my works have never been meant as pasquils or pamphlets aimed at any particular political system (not at least as a general rule). Instead I would see myself somewhat like a mathematician or a composer of music. I wrote my works from a perspective intended to bypass all Marxist censors, simply because I would move about in philosophical and futurological domains where they had nothing to say.

It was different, of course, in Stalin's times. During the classic, hard-core Stalinism before the political thaw of the 1960s, even so innocent a book as *The Astronauts* came under fire. I had a meeting, or rather a head-on collision, with the Russian translators, during which they demanded that I make hundreds of revisions before *The Astronauts* could be published in Russia. Since I would not budge an inch, it took a little time, a year or two perhaps, but eventually the novel got published. At that point, of course, it turned out that nobody paid any attention to these alleged monstrous heresies of mine.

Swirski: *When writing about Bellow's* Mr. Sammler's Planet *you complained that, in his description of the occupation experience, Bellow did not get the mood and the details right. Elsewhere you leveled the same charge against Kosinski's* Painted Bird. *His description of the German occupation of Poland also left much to be desired. Could you comment on the relation between fact and fiction in literary works?*

Lem: With Kosinski it was the sexual promiscuity of the Polish peasantry that was most objectionable. He reinvented the Polish countryside as a place where everyone was fixated on quenching their sexual appetites. For anyone who knows this country and things as they really were, this seems a patent lunacy. Yet it was a gimmick that worked for him. Still, solid sociological experience does not always end up being utilized by writers of fiction. As for Bellow, in *Mr. Sammler's Planet* he tried hard to describe the conditions in occupied Poland. But there are these minute, even if difficult to pinpoint, details that allow readers like myself to sense that he was not himself a participant in these calamitous events, that he was writing from secondhand experience, so to say.

A reconstruction of events is a complicated process even in the best of times. Over the years there were, to take one example, countless efforts to reconstruct what the giant Jurassic lizards looked and behaved like. There were conjectures that they moved rather slowly, that their tails trailed on the ground. Then, on the basis of some equivocally interpretable markings on some skeletal fragments, another school of scientists concluded that they were actually agile and rapid movers, that their tails must have been more sinewy and rigid than previously thought, that they looked more like bipedal birds, with the raised tail used for counterbalance, and so on.

Clearly, from a collection of elementary building blocks one can piece together various interpretations of a given phenomenon. On the other hand, no one will ever go back to the Jurassic times to film a live giant reptile, and thus we will never have conclusive evidence to prove how things really were back then. This is clearly a fundamental difference, because if someone has lived through the concentration camps, or through the wartime occupation of Poland, or even, as the case may be, through a form of underground resistance as I did, then his experience is irrefutable, simply because it is authentic. Someone else, forced to work with historical accounts of these horrors, might invent a plausible plot which would nevertheless lack something vital.

Let me give you an example of what I have in mind. Several years ago, in 1986, a Polish writer, Andrzej Szczypiorski, wrote a novel called *Początek* [*The Beginning*] which later, under a different title [*The Beautiful Mrs. Seidenman*], became a runaway best-seller in Europe. What was so special about it? Up until that point writers constructed war narratives around various intersecting human lives, with the German occupation as a historical backdrop. This man took the whole thing much further, right into the heart of postwar communist Poland. In his novel, if someone had been a collaborator and a Jew-hater during the war, he would end up as an orthodox communist, with a cosy sinecure as a director of a state company, or something like that. In this way the author modeled some aspects of transition from one political formation into another, a subject from applied sociology which had for the longest time been covered by a veil of silence.

Swirski: *How then are we to judge the sociological contribution of a work of fiction?*

Lem: The starting question must be whether we are facing a literary work that positions itself within the conventions of classical narrative realism. For example, if there was a way to group Bellow's work with the school of the French New Novel, then everything in *Mr. Sammler's Planet* would automatically become possible. All objections about missing elements and lack of semblance to reality, articulated from the realistic standpoint and in the spirit of historiographic accuracy, would lose their argumentative ground, since in the *Nouveau roman* anything goes, as it were. This is of course a vexing situation for literary critics and scholars.

A friend of mine, an American writer who lives in Vienna, recently wrote a novel with elements of magic, fantasy, and the supernatural. The whole thing takes place somewhere in occupied France, I think; there are Jewish children who are to be taken to the gas chamber, but then a magician arrives and helps these children fly out of a window like little angels. The reason I did not enjoy this book was because I know that the fate of such children was quite the opposite: they ended up dead in the gas chamber, not flying away to freedom. Naturally, I understand and recognize the literary convention, as well as the noble intentions of the author, who wished—for the sake of his readers as well as these children—to spare them from the inhuman cruelty of war. However, we cannot afford to be spared from reality, no matter how cruel, if we are to remain in the categories of the real world.

Incidentally, this reminds me of the famous scene from Andrzej Wajda's film *Korczak,* where—note the analogy—condemned children, led by Korczak, leave the train cars in which they were to be taken away. In France, when the movie was released, there was a terrible uproar over this scene; everybody got mad at the director. I must admit I also have my reservations. I am not dogmatic about it, but a priori I am of the opinion that such a fusion of genres, blending a bit of realism here with a bit of fairy tale there, is not the best thing.

Swirski: *You seem to consider the cognitive value of a literary work in literal rather than symbolic terms. Yet a work of fiction can be absolutely nonrealistic but have a great deal of cognitive value. The modeling value of fiction is, to some degree at least, independent of narrative conventions. Thus genre "inbreeding" can hardly be condemned outright as undesirable.*

Lem: What I regard as improper is what I called once "generic incest," that is, where a part of a work is written according to the conventions of realism, while the rest is written in an antiveristic mode. For example, first we get the reality of wartime occupation of Poland—harrowing experience, described in convincing detail—and then somebody grows wings and flies out of the window. If everybody in the novel had wings and used them to fly, right from the start, there would be no problem. If magic is an integral part of the design of the narrative, everything is fine. But the arbitrary mixing that we actually get is difficult to accept. This matter could also be analyzed in terms of the author's executive strategy, considered from the point of view of game theory. When we play bridge I am not allowed all of a sudden to pull out an extra fifth ace, announce I have a trump, and proceed to trounce everybody with it.

Everyone knows that one cannot fry a wristwatch in butter as if it was an egg. Yet Salvador Dali did just that; you can see his watch-omelets and other concoctions. This is the prerogative of surrealism: once we enter its dimension, everything becomes possible. It is purely a matter of modality. If I write a work like *The Cyberiad*, the criteria of realism do not apply in it in any sense. Take the scene where my two robot protagonists herd in together a number of stars, in order to make out of them a cosmic advertising sign. This is pure fairy tale.

The cognitive value of *The Cyberiad* resides on another plane, not on the literal plane of the depicted events. Of course, we encounter here a problem of another type, because we could never designate a closed and countable set of all the rules which must be observed so that the literary game can be played out properly (this is, incidentally, why literary metacriticism is a philosophical enterprise of such daunting proportions). The moment that failure to observe some rule can bring about a positive outcome in the artistic sense, not even classic game theory can be of any help.

Swirski: *Since you mentioned game theory, do you think it could help us in modeling interpretive strategies employed by readers of literary works? For example, a feeling of artistic excellence experienced by readers/critics could, under some conditions (for example, those specified by Luce and Raiffa in* Games and Decisions*),[1] be expressed as a utility function. Do you think we could use this procedure—as it is used in decision theory or game theory—to help in understanding, interpreting, or perhaps even evaluating literary works?*

Lem: To tell you the truth, I am skeptical to the highest degree that something like that should ever become possible. Think of all those dishes on the menu in any good Chinese restaurant. I do not believe that it will ever be possible to represent the taste of any dish in words, or in some information-carrying signs, in a way that would allow a person who had never tasted it to recognize it from among a score of others on the basis of this information alone. It is out of the question; it is simply impossible to translate such experiences or perceptions into language.

Comparisons are always possible, that is true. My question is, however, so what? Literary experience does indeed provide a form of information, but it is neither quantifiable nor universally accessible. Based on my experience as a reader and author, I am convinced that it is impossible to design a coherent metaliterary model which would authorize only a unique type of creativity or criticism. Optimal strategies of literary interpretation never exist uniquely, but come in interrelated and correlated sets. It is pretty much the same with translations. There are several different Polish translations of Shakespeare, most of them very good, yet not only are they not identical, but in fact quite divergent. And there is no way to avoid this. Some readers will always like this translation of *Hamlet,* while others will find a different one much more congenial.

As far as axiology is concerned, some evaluative criteria are always in place during our encounters with literature. And perhaps these same criteria could be somehow quantified or analyzed, perhaps using the tools of game theory. Yet nobody cares to try it since this is already a subject for the sociology of literature. In the past, when I thought of ways of tackling this problem, I imagined you could do it like this. Take a group of people which is sizable enough to be statistically meaningful (let us say about fifty strong), and fairly representative of the reading elite of a given society. Then—if I can put it this way—run various works through that group, using them as a sort of literary "filter." To be precise: people in the group will read the works that you supply them with, each with a ranking list that goes, let's say, from minus to plus ten. Ten denotes a work of the highest caliber, minus ten the worst one.

Now, even though I have never run such an experiment, I am sure that once you accumulate this statistical material, you will see a greater divergence of views than you could imagine. Of course, it is important in the experiment to give them only books which they have not read before, otherwise they would be aware in advance that Dostoevsky is a famous author, and that Agatha Christie is not in his class. So they should read only books which would be completely new to them, and without knowing the name of the author. In the end it would also turn out, I suspect, that the more sophisticated and representative this elite group, the greater would be the divergence between the works which these experts would recognize as good and those they would rank as terrible. Naturally, there would be discrepancies, but the larger the statistical sample, the more these discrepancies would be "smoothed out." This is all said, of course, with the understanding that these evaluations would be sound only statistically, and that the opinion of any single expert, however eminent, could be dangerously fallible. Edmund Wilson, the English critic, was a good friend of Nabokov's, and yet he thought *Lolita* was worthless.

Swirski: *From a game theoretic point of view, you approach the interaction between the "players" in a literary "game" not in terms of two individuals, but as an individual (the author) confronting a collection or community of readers, considered as a single player.*

Lem: You know, the decision as to which type of model best describes the situation is a tricky issue, and depends to a considerable degree on a number of pragmatic factors which are infrequently mentioned, if at all. Take only one example. There are types of information that precede and thus influence the process of reading, for example, the name of the publisher, the year of printing, the country where the book came out, and so on. We are involved here in a tangle of factors the role of which could not possibly be calculated in advance.

When we are instructed that we are going to listen to a musical work found posthumously in the papers of Johann Sebastian Bach, our sense of anticipation is enormous. But when we are told that it is, in fact, only a suite composed by a postman from Scarborough, the situation becomes markedly different. In the case of the postman we are no longer so prepared to honor the work. One hears sometimes about a discovery of a bunch of letters, apparently of little consequence, but once it is established that they were written by Chopin then, my God, everybody starts to approach them with reverence. By the same token, if I was a famous cook who never wrote a literary work in his life, you would hardly even think of trying to get me to talk about literature. For all you know, you might get a culinary recipe out of me for your trouble.

I am familiar with a lot of work from applied cybernetics—applied to the field of literature, that is. One should not believe too much in what these scholars have to say, in their equations, theorems, and so on. This is all wishful thinking. As you know, there were hypotheses advanced in the field that the essence of the literary interpretive process could be captured by the idea of maximizing information. Thus if you get four megabytes out of a literary work, and somebody else gets only two, then your standing as a reader should be twice as good as his—this is all patent nonsense.

First of all, no one could ever know how many megabytes you got out of your reading because, as a reader, you input and read many things *into* the text. Second, although I am anything but a Freudian or a psychoanalyst, I am persuaded that there exists something like the subconscious in the mind of the author. And so, even though one can apply certain insights and methods of game theory to reflect on various strategies of reception, ultimately it will always be conjectural work. This is not unlike arriving at the scene of the crime with a magnifying glass, like Sherlock Holmes, and having to read a posteriori from the clues what had happened. There is simply no other way—to some degree it will always be a form of reconstruction, like with the Jurassic reptile fossils. And within such readerly, critical, or metacritical reconstructive work there is no room for ultimate precision and unity, or for believing one's interpretation to be the true and only one.

There is one other factor, very amusing and quite irrational at the bottom. I know that I have some die-hard enemies, who hate me for my views on the sorry state of their literary productions. All the same, they can all see by the fact that I keep getting published, reprinted, reviewed, studied, and honored with literary awards, that there is no getting rid of me, that I am here to stay. Quite simply, the longer a writer survives within the world of art, the more his longevity works for him in terms of acceptance and recognition. This is completely irrational, because books do not become better just because they are endlessly reprinted. It would be nonsense to claim that since Lem gets reprinted, his books must be good (in fact, if anything, the relation must be just the reverse).

To tell you the truth, I have always suspected that 95 percent of people who shell out millions for a Picasso, don't really see anything in his paintings at all. It is simply a form of capital investment which allows the buyer to stake out a claim to being a connoisseur. Much in the same way there is plenty of pretense in the domain of literature and its reception. We can easily identify some very typical processes at work. For example, it is certainly not true that best-sellers are always the most widely read books. They are merely most frequently bought, and surely this is not the same thing. Here is a typical real life story, related to me by a friend from Los Angeles. A woman walks into a book store and demands a book that tops the best-seller list. The shop assistant informs her that they are out, and suggests a number two instead. "I never buy anything but number one," replies the woman and leaves the store. This is exactly the kind of attitude I am talking about, but here again we have already entered the realm of the sociology of literature.

There are also the *genius loci* and *genius tempori,* inscrutable yet always present, two subtle pragmatic factors which one must never forget when talking about strategies of reception. They are a kind of codeterminant, a coefficient that involves what can only be called a favorable configuration of pragmatic circumstances surrounding the publication of the work—call it luck, if you will. It means that there is a kind of resonance in the reading public, which, like an acoustic guitar, resonates with the content of a work and amplifies it. The vital role of this last element is immediately evident in the cases when it is absent: without such resonance a work dies without a trace. This is similar to a nuclear chain reaction. In the ordinary, not enriched isotope of uranium 235, there are some free neutrons going around, but not enough to bring the whole pile to any kind of explosion. However, if you enrich the weapons-grade isotope past a certain level, you will reach the critical mass where the neutron breeding coefficient becomes greater than one, and the whole thing blows up. This is the typical situation of a book which becomes a best-seller.

Speaking of best-sellers, most of them obviously enjoy only a very short life. There are people who, as a rule, tend to be rather negatively biased toward such literary supernovas. For instance, my friend Slawomir Mrozek refused to read Umberto Eco's *Name of the Rose* when it was so popular. I actually had to persuade him in my correspondence to read it, arguing that this was one of those infrequent exceptions to the rule that every best-seller must be trash. In the end he read it and admitted that I had been right. Again, this is to show that there are many pitfalls lying along our way, many places where the reader and critic can easily be led astray. But, as students of objectivity and the rational method, we must not overlook them just because they are a bit more messy than what we are used to in literary studies.

There is no getting around pragmatics in trying to account fully for the perceptual and emotional experience of reading. Let me get to it through a quote from Witold Gombrowicz. Once, irritated, Gombrowicz wrote in his diary: "What is this? Young people write books so that I, an old man, should read them? Ha," he said, "to write a book is nothing. To make others read it, this is a true art." Of course this is quite aphoristic, but at the same time hits the nail right on the head.

I have had many more offers and invitations than I could ever realize in a lifetime. I get phone calls all the time, asking me to fly to this or that conference, give a speech, a lecture, and so on. And all I can say is, you should have asked me twenty-five years ago; now it is too late. But they persist, a 100,000 deutsche marks on the table and an open invitation to write a book for a publisher in Germany. My editions in Germany are staggering; I am not even sure exactly why it is so. So I ask, "All right, but what kind of book are we talking about here? A phone book from Mars?" No sweat, it does not matter, anything as long as my name is on its cover—whatever "it" may turn out to be.

This is just the same as with the Mercedes or Cadillac trademark. What is more important than the particular literary work that gets promoted and sold, is the trademark that generates the sales. I happen to be such a popular and recognizable trademark. We are talking here about the commercialization of the entire publishing enterprise. Initially Faber and Faber did not even want to publish my *Solaris* at all, and now? There are leather-bound editions of *The Cyberiad* priced at seventy-five dollars for the collectors and lovers of my works, looking more like the Bible than anything else: quality paper, leather, gilt letters, the works.

These pragmatic circumstances can change the picture for the reader and the critic in dramatic ways. But why care for literature in the first place? Today we are incessantly bombarded with messages that literature is dead—the equivalent of obsequies performed at the side of the literary grave. Nobody has the patience to read any more, we are told; the visual arts have dealt literature a mortal blow. True enough: we have forty-odd television channels, and soon in Europe alone there will be two hundred. This is simply appalling. It is like having two thousand shirts or pairs of shoes. Can anyone who owns two thousand pairs of shoes wear a different pair each day? But then he will never break them in and his feet will be forever covered in blisters! This is informational nonsense.

Swirski: *But literature performs, or ought to perform, a different function than television and cinema. It does not make sense to compete with the visual media in terms of image and picture in the first place, and such competition strikes me as an enforced one. Literature has other roles to play in the society—for example, cognitive.*

Lem: Cognition? Look at the way television series are put together. The stories are assembled from a minimum number of situation/plot building blocks, and this pattern is consciously replicated (never mind the lost potential for richness and originality). The same thing can be observed in the case of literary works which have proven to be successful. Legions of writers follow the trail broken by the forerunner, widening and domesticating it with dozens of stories which all try to emulate the winner. We live in the era of mass culture, you know, and we must not dwell in the elitist stratosphere where we lose sight of the entire panorama below, including literature which inhabits the regions very close to ground zero.

Coming back to readers of fiction and the indeterminacy of interpretive strategies, we must keep in mind that a strategy of reception is not something that is adopted with full deliberation. A normal reader does not even know exactly how he goes about his interpretive business. Take an average person who is fluent in his own native tongue, and ask him how it is possible that he speaks it without knowing the grammar. He won't tell you because he does not know it himself. Reading a book is the same thing.

The average reader applies a certain strategy of reception without even being aware that it is a strategy of reception. This is the process which the theorists who study metaliterary matters try to model, by bringing it up to the conscious level. Still, so many theories of literary works have come to light that the field begins to resemble the Tower of Babel. On top of this terrible proliferation, there are ephemeral trends and fashions: structuralism, postmodernism, deconstruction, new historicism.

Let us remember that, even though all theories, by their intrinsic nature, are simplifications in relation to what they describe, the approximations in literary studies are too crude not to be superficial. Naturally the situation is a little different in the literary, as opposed to metaliterary, domain. You will never succeed in building a car without proper theory, but you can write fiction without the foggiest idea of what literary theory is. When I wrote my own works, God forbid that I should have ever thought of theory. These matters are all located at separate addresses in our heads. I remember, back in Lvov, when I was twelve, I got my first pair of skis from my father, together with a book written by this phenomenal Swedish skiing specialist, so that by the time I put the skis on, I had the whole theory in my little finger. And still I wiped out on my first try! The theory was there but it did not help me much in practice. With literature the situation is identical: theory is not equivalent to practice.

On the other hand, even though to be an excellent writer one does not have to be a university graduate, still one must be predisposed to it in certain ways. It would be difficult to define these attributes precisely, but some should be obvious: a thoughtful and reflexive nature, disregard for the allure of making money, and so on. Take my own example: I do not know if I could write a book deliberately pandering to the tastes of the general public. In my career as a writer I had several runaway best-sellers in Europe. Yet I never wrote them after deliberating about what kind of reader I was aiming at. This kind of question is put to me at every occasion, and my answer is always the same: I never gave any thought at all to the question of who my "target" or "virtual" reader may have been. I wrote about what interested me, so in that sense I wrote for myself.

I still have the knack for plot and storyline, but I lost the drive and the interest for it. I realize now how many people buy books just because other people buy them, so why should I sweat and toil? Despite staggering figures of books in print, the number of works worth reading is exceedingly limited. I returned recently from Vienna where I collected a major literary award; I visited many bookstores there, all of them packed with the printed word to the point of bursting, but I could rarely find more than just a couple of books to buy, and sometimes literally nothing at all.

All this is to say that problems of interpreting literature are immersed in this vast indeterminacy that is not unlike the haze surrounding the sphere of erotic relations between men and women. I sometimes use the latter as a metaphor in discussions about literature, because these matters are also not easy to articulate. These days the literary market is inundated with hundreds of guides to sexual technique, but this has precious little to do with true love. Can someone really believe that the most skilled lover in the world is also the best, or that one can fall in love and be able to explain precisely why? To make a long story short, there are pragmatic elements involved in the interpretation of processes that relate to personal experience, which most scholars sweep under the theoretical carpet.

Swirski: *You suggested that for individual readers one could indeed derive a utility function that might predict with some accuracy their response to and evaluation of works of literature. Could we extend this process to groups or even communities of readers?*

Lem: In some circumstances, it could indeed be possible to establish the probability of a given literary work's success. We could call it "virtual" popularity, that is, we wouldn't know for sure that it would happen, but it should be quite likely. One thing that we must keep in mind here is that, in order to improve diagnostic accuracy, we would always have to withhold the names of the authors. If the reader knew the author and liked him, he would already be positively biased. And what we are after is the maximum absence of bias.

The information that precedes reading, the information that attracts people to reading, the information that determines the selection of one work over another, are all types of information that are not internal with regard to the text, but external. This external superstructure is very important. I know it from my own experience with the reception of my *Memoirs Found in a Bathtub*. When my agent mailed it off to a press in Germany, the manuscript came back after four weeks with a comment that it was worthless, and that the publisher saw absolutely no merit in it. This manuscript went subsequently from one publisher to another for a long time, since my agent was an obstinate man who would not take no for an answer. At last, with great difficulties, *Memoirs* came out in print in Germany. Today I can't even remember how many editions this novel had in the years to follow. There were ordinary editions, special club editions, everybody would talk about the book with excitement and enthusiasm, and it was most interesting to hear how good it was, sometimes from the same people who had rejected it before, in most cases not without having read it!

The whole thing is actually quite typical. The work had not been preceded by any commending information. It was not a recently discovered manuscript by Kafka but a novel written by some guy called Lem. Such peripeties are often glossed over by the history of literature in silence. Maybe literary critics find it awkward to talk about such stunning contradictions in interpretation and reception. I even asked various theoreticians how it was possible to have such differences of opinion—first negative, adulatory later—but nobody could tell me anything that made sense.

It was no different with Nabokov's *Lolita*. The critics shrugged it off, saying it was pornography or, even worse, that it was nothing at all. The first edition was with some fourth-rate publisher of suspect credentials. And then? An explosion of acceptance and enthusiasm, elevation to a different social level, a change in the stratification of reception, and eventually a world career. They made it into a movie, then another, and then this single work which made it so big became an "elevator" which pulled all of Nabokov's other books out of nonexistence. Now he is well known, respected, there are master's theses, even doctoral studies on his subject— no one knows where it is going to end. What kind of enthusiasm is it, though, which arrives with a delay of so many years? I find it hard to credit such belated excitement with genuineness and authenticity.

There are many professional mysteries buried in the field of literary criticism. To begin, it is obviously not true that all this is a kind of conspiracy, a collusion among miscreants who claim to be critics. Also, it makes no sense to argue that no one ever bothers to read anything, that all reviewed material is tossed straight out of the window—before reading, that is. Maybe the charge would stick with one critic or two, or even three perhaps, but not with all without exception.

But here again we are back to statistics, which make everything so very difficult. In general, we could say that, when one reads a literary work that is significantly original, the reading experience is rarely one of unmitigated ease. Kafka himself published very little in his lifetime, and even pleaded with Max Brod to burn all of his manuscripts, because no one would read them. It would seem that an unrecognized literary work is like a safe to which nobody knows the opening sequence. One only has to discover the sequence which cracks the safe open to make it reveal all of its treasures. Now, as a metaphor this is actually quite evocative, but how does it actually work?

The fates of books are frequently tortuous and peculiar, and the history of literature from the perspective I am emphasizing depends in a large measure on refraining from talking about it—the less the better. In high society one does not stoop to discussing wetting one's pants, and what we get from literary history are high-society legends. Why insist on remembering that Kafka was completely forgotten during his lifetime, that no one would read his books, that they used to tell him, "What kind of idiocies are these?" Let us not forget that he did not even finish *The Castle*. The same with Robert Musil; Thomas Mann himself penned superlative reviews of Musil's work, and to what effect? Nobody would read Musil anyway. And later? Musil the great writer, Musil the great Austrian. . . . There are things which, as critics, scholars, and literary historians, we must never forget, and among them are the phenomena of chance and luck. I suggest that, in general, the model which reflects the situation is one of random interaction, where a work of literature is a Brownian molecule whose contact with another molecule means that it finds a reader.

Swirski: *In view of noticeable resistance to, and even cultivated ignorance of, philosophy and science in literary studies, what role do you think other disciplines could play in the humanistic and literary fields?*

Lem: I think that methodological approaches grounded in concrete theories from outside the humanities are very tempting on one hand and very risky on the other. To be completely frank, we do not have in the humanities, and particularly in literary studies, any tools which could apply some kind of axiological "barometer" to a literary work and allow us to detect its various qualities, in the same way that the reader experiences them while reading. This is, of course, only one of the difficulties we face. We have what is called a "macro" approach, whereas all the other facets of the work are left unaccounted for.

It is for this reason that I took structuralism to task in my various works on literary theory. In some demented democratic way, structuralism equalized the structures of first- and third-rate works since, in terms of its methodology, they were all the same. Of course this goes all the way back to Claude Lévi-Strauss and one of his fundamental theses about the equality of different human cultures. For Lévi-Strauss there were no superior and inferior cultures, and this ideological and methodological view automatically places all cultural phenomena on the same footing. On the other hand, if one were to approach Agatha Christie and Dostoevsky as writers of crime fiction, distinguishable only by some nuance of style, any honest critic and connoisseur would write it off as heresy and nonsense. Yet, if one examines them purely in terms of plot and structure, *Crime and Punishment* and a novel by Christie have indeed much in common. Such an approach, however, neglects the socio-aesthetic problems and nuances that actually bring literature to life. This is exactly the reason why I resisted structuralism when it was still the rage (now it is defunct on its own merit, dying the natural death of all transient fashions).

Swirski: *In* Philosophy of Chance *you point to game theory as a promising tool in literary studies. Could you comment on it now, from the perspective of twenty-five years?*

Lem: Unlike the sciences, the humanities are characterized by a lack of cumulativeness in their search for knowledge. In this respect they resemble the domain of fashion, with only appearances of exactness in their methods. I applied comparatively some elements of game theory to the works of the Marquis de Sade in "Markiz w grafie" ("The Marquis in a Graph," 1979). This extensive study brought me a lot of satisfaction, just because I proved to myself that it could be done. The funny thing about it was that I had initially no interest in writing about de Sade. It was actually the reverse. I was studying the differences between utopia, science fiction, and fairy tale, and the game theoretic schema which I devised for literary zero-sum and nonzero-sum games indicated a narrative "empty spot." This unoccupied place in my system was reserved for an anti–fairy tale. Mark Twain wrote once such anti–fairy tales: in them the nicest boys always end up the worst, virtue is always rewarded with the harshest punishment, and so on. I was quite intrigued by all this, and I started to ponder what this anti–fairy tale—in which evil always wins, and where evil is a virtue pursued by the hero—might look like. And it turned out that this was exactly Marquis de Sade.

Of course, this type of analysis is not axiological per se. In my essay I was after something else. I became interested in determining what values may be dominant in writers' intentions, and how these values could be captured in a game theoretic schema describing particular works and genres. Take fairy tale as an example. The genre represents a kind of literary space in which the laws of physics are subordinate to another type of law. This is fairy tale's internal axiology. It does not allow accidents which would be inimical to the protagonist. It is impossible that the hero who fights the dragon should slip on a banana peel and, as a result, get eaten alive. But, on the other hand, in de Sade's *Justine: ou les malheurs de la virtu,* when the poor girl runs away during a thunderstorm, after being repeatedly raped and abused, she gets struck by a bolt of lightning.

Naturally we can find in de Sade a number of antinomies, owing to the fact that he was—at least for his times—an atheist, while at the same time bearing a terrible hatred toward God. As hard as it is to hate God, while at the same time insisting that he does not exist—that's de Sade for you. In other of my studies I questioned the relatively high esteem he enjoys. He is really an exceptional phenomenon, since his works do not have much intrinsic appeal in terms of artistic excellence, only as an example of a certain extremism—as an example of anti–fairy tale.

De Sade is a classic apologist of Evil. For him Evil is something so magnificent that perpetrating it is utterly delectable. All historically infamous perpetrators of evil have almost without exception referred to it as a kind of necessity, which may have brought suffering and pain, but which was carried out in the service of a higher Good. It was, after all, for the good of the German nation that Hitler was going to slaughter the Slavs and the Jews. Stalin, too, exterminated in the name of the splendid future. This is how it usually works. But a defense of Evil which praises and elevates it—this you do not find too often. The exceptional status and the historical context of the "divine Marquis" is responsible for the regard he commands from the critics as a writer worthy of close scrutiny. For myself, I was rather surprised that, using certain concepts from game theory, I was able to reach de Sade through a comparative analysis of various literary genres.

Most of the games taking place in fairy tale are, of course, of the zero-sum type, even though one could never hope to quantify them. You can't say, for example, that when the protagonist awakens a sleeping beauty, or liberates her from the castle of a malevolent witch, he gains precisely as much as the witch loses. There is no way in the world to calculate that. And yet, in the commonsensical perception of the reader, justice is being done. In other words, we have a zero-sum symmetry: first something bad happens, some sort of disruption of harmony of existence, which afterward gets corrected, so that everything is back in order again. In contrast, in de Sade we witness the persecution of hapless victims. The more a saint and a virgin, the more terrible things must befall the girl, the more cruel treatment she must undergo at the hands of villains. This is not a zero-sum game, for we can no longer argue at this point that there is some kind of compensatory force at work.

Another thing to consider are the *logical* consequences of the narrative, in contrast to the ends demanded by more literary (aesthetic) considerations. In de Sade you get the evilmost monster of all, who has murdered, raped, and slaughtered everybody else, so that he alone remains in the field of corpses. This protagonist finds himself suddenly in a state of insatiability since his raison d'être is to perpetrate evil, and now there is no one left around for him to persecute. A suicide, of course, would be no solution. In other words, the situation changes from a zero-sum game to nonzero-sum.

In addition there is also the question of utopia, in which we are dealing not with an individual protagonist but with an entire society that achieves happiness. That actually got me to think about ways in which one could interpret utopia in game theoretic terms. In the end I realized that, since utopia is an unsurpassably perfect state, there is no room in it for any active strategy in the absence of an opponent.

Swirski: *Utopia can be seen as the terminal phase of a conflict that has taken place, as it were, before the narrative time of the novel. In other words classical utopia would be a phase where the players—the society—collect their winnings.*

Lem: Yes, one must distinguish the classical from the modern utopia. The moment that modern-day political fiction and science fiction entered the picture, the whole genre picture became much more messy and intractable. Anyway, I clearly did not concern myself with which fairy tales are better and which are worse, because game theoretic tools do not provide any criteria of differentiation for this task. What I was after was the genre schema, which I published under a somewhat amusing name of "Markiz w grafie" ("The Marquis in a Graph"). The title is an allusion to game theory, strategy selection process, binary trees, and the like, which I actually used in the text. Still, this is a rather isolated work in my opus since I have not been involved in literary criticism and theory in a systematic way.

Jerzy Jarzebski, a specialist in Polish literature, is in the process of writing his second book about me (the first one was published only in German as *Zufall und Ordnung* [*Chance and Order*]). As a specialist from the humanities, he ran into typical difficulties when writing about me, since what is integral to my writings is often ill-suited to critical analysis conducted from a purely literary perspective. This is because my works frequently contain a cognitive, or prognostic-futurological component, which de facto lies outside the scope of traditional literary studies.

Speaking of prognostication and futurology—of my nonfiction I regard *Summa technologiae* as a remarkably successful book, in the sense that so much of what I wrote there has in the meantime come true. This is all the more remarkable since, during the time when I was writing it, I had almost no access to professional futurological literature. Although the concept of futurology had been worked out by Ossip Flechtheim all the way back in 1942, I did not know anything about it, since I was isolated from relevant publications. Futurology became trendy and popular a few years after the publication of *Summa,* which had an edition of three thousand copies and was scrupulously overlooked in Poland by all reviewers, with the exception of a single devastating critique by Leszek Kolakowski. He laughed at me, and wrote that I behaved like a boy in a sandbox who, just because he has a toy spade in his hands, thinks he can dig right through to the other side of the Earth. Thirty years after his critique, I wrote a substantial rebuttal in the form of an essay entitled "Thirty Years Later," which reports on what has come true of my predictions and hypotheses from *Summa.*

In the article I could not, for obvious reasons, make references to the whole book, so instead I focused on the chapter devoted to phantomatics, with the idea of confronting my theories and their contemporary position with what Kolakowski had to say about them in his original review. I wrote *Summa* in the 1960s, when I had no access to relevant information. If I had an abundance of it, as I do now, I probably would not have dared to. I would have known about the Rand Corporation and the Hudson Institute, with Herman Kahn and hundreds of his collaborators with their computers, an all-knowing bunch of specialists with the CIA archives at their disposal, where they could look up all kinds of information—both true and false, as it turned out on their assessment of the economic strength of the Soviet Union. In 1990, for instance, they still ranked it second, after the U.S. but before Japan, whereas everyone knows what the former Soviet empire looks like today. In the 1960s I was completely unaware of all this; today, if I were to write *Summa* all over again, the situation would be different.

I have stacks of unopened deliveries from the magazine *New Science,* which arrive to my address as regularly as a metronome, one every week, fifty-two a year. I decided to cancel my subscription—I am simply unable to keep up. Paradoxically, an excess of information can paralyze as effectively as its absence. In order to cope with it, one would have to employ dozens of experts as a kind of "information filter." So, as far as *Summa* is concerned, paradoxical situations can sometimes give rise to original and valuable philosophical studies (the same actually applies to my literary fictions).

Swirski: *At several points in* Summa *you discuss the concept of "black box" machines, which also returns in a couple of your novels, namely as the ocean in* Solaris *and the Black Cloud in* The Invincible. *Since the concept seemed quite important in your nonfiction, it would seem that the novelistic description of these systems should have been developed with great detail, perhaps by having the agents study them or try to harness them technologically. Yet, instead, your Kelvins and Horpaches walk away, foregoing the chance to explore the idea of the black box machine further. Since this could be considered a cognitive shortcoming of these novels, why don't your agents ever attempt to understand and exploit the regularities of these black boxes, as any proper investigator and scientist should do? In other words, why did you not develop this concept with similar precision in your fiction as you did in your nonfiction?*

Lem: By chance I was flipping today through a recent issue of *Newsweek,* in which I found an article about a British scientist who recently took up writing what can only be described as science fiction. However, as the article makes clear, he resists such a classification of his work, just because he believes that it brings him absolutely no literary merit. He has written a couple of books; one of them is about a fictive discovery of the cause of cancer; the other is a story about the famous French group of anonymous mathematicians. What is interesting about this latter work is that it ends without a solution to the problem it sets up. This is a deliberate move on the author's part, which reminds me of several of my own fictions (of course he arrived at this idea independently of me).

No matter what domain of human inquiry we might consider, there are no unequivocal solutions in black and white. The conviction, often entertained by humanists, that in the hard sciences (e.g., physics) everything must be lucid and transparent, simply does not correspond to reality. This is not only because there are endless controversies in physics just as in anything else, but because the pinnacle of human cognition simply does not exist. The sciences are always in the process of climbing toward those peaks of knowledge that are hidden above the clouds, making errors as they go. The only systems that can pronounce their infallibility are religious dogmas, as well as some forms of ideology, like Marxism. The contrast between these last two is that as soon as Marxism was brought into confrontation with life and reality, it began to crumble and break, with the consequences visible in what used to be the communist camp.

My philosophical affiliation, if I were to put it in terms of accepted nomenclature, is in a large measure with the skeptics. I am not given to prostrating myself before the natural sciences, and I have frequently adopted quite an irreverent attitude toward them in my stories. Lying on my desk is a book called *Errors of Science*. It describes deceptions committed by scientists in their research. The author, an expert in the subject, makes no bones about the fact that there is a tremendous amount of material to write about. The hostilities between the French and the Americans about who first isolated the AIDS virus, the insane combats around Nobel Prizes—examples can be multiplied hundredfold. Sociology of science shows that scientists are, above all, human beings just like the rest of us, with the same kinds of passions, open in the same ways to error or craving for power.

However, to come back to our issue: the majority of my books—here *The Investigation* can be a paradigmatic example—never settle for easy solutions, always keeping the mystery open till the end. The way I feel about it, the task of a writer is not to dish out quick and easy recipes for ultimate solutions, but to signal certain problems and pose questions about them. This is, of course, completely unlike the crime novels which so many people like to read (and I am one of them).

Swirski: *All the same, after reading* Solaris *and* The Invincible, *the feeling remains that some further action by the explorers is called for. No longer efforts at communication with the "sentient systems"—here I am in complete agreement with you—but precisely the type of action that would be consistent with the narrative makeup of the agents who are, after all, scientists and not conquistadors. I am aware that I may sound like I want to rewrite your works, but both novels leave the impression that they should continue past their present end. The first exploratory phase is over, we have come to recognize our conceptual insufficiencies, the skepticism of which you just spoke is now in place, so let's go and have some decent studies of these baffling systems, right?*

Lem: OK, it could be done, but I would argue that in epistemological terms it would have been sterile, and in narrative terms hardly interesting. I must admit that I was myself a little uncomfortable with the total insolubility of the mystery of the moving corpses in *The Investigation*. I was aware that I had broken the conventions of a typical crime novel, which actually moved me years later to write *The Chain of Chance*, in which everything is brought to a conclusion. It was an alternative treatment of the same problem as in *The Investigation;* only this time the culprit, and thus the vehicle for the plot, are identified as chance and multiple coincidence. So, I think that I can understand the critique of *The Investigation* from a purely epistemic and cognitive angle.

At the same time, the set of readers who were fascinated by these two works splits right down the middle, and whereas one group regards *The Investigation* as superior because the mystery remains unresolved, the other prefers *The Chain of Chance* precisely because there the enigma is solved. If we were to consider the matter from a cognitive point of view, it is no doubt always preferable to know the causes of events, but when we consider the reception of a work of literature, the lack of resolution and the openness of the mystery has its own merit as well.

All of this, however, was not conceived deliberately, that is, it was not a malicious premeditation on my part to taunt the reader with an unsolved mystery. When I write I don't know in advance whether the mystery will be solved or not. This is because—as I have said before on numerous occasions—I never plan things ahead, but rather wait to see how the narrative shapes up. I am like a coachman, to a certain degree in control of my material, but even I can't make the cab take off to the air or make the horses run as fast as a plane.

Swirski: *Your novels as well as* Summa *were written more or less at the same time. In* Summa *you raise the prospect of a study and development of black box technology, yet your fictional scientists walk away from intriguing black box systems, even though the technological might of the ocean and the Cloud clearly outstrips human knowledge. The novels end just as the real philosophical and narrative challenge appears on the horizon. How about developing these works beyond their present shape? Perhaps writing a* Solaris Part 2 *where humans utilize the abilities of the "neutrino phantoms," for example, where humans explore space in the company of phantom crews. These creatures are, after all, stronger, more resilient, they don't need to eat—ideal for the job.*

Lem: Let me tell you something which on the surface may appear to have no direct relation to what you just said. The one area of knowledge which was most influential in my learning process as a writer—not just in the literary, but in a general philosophical sense—was the natural sciences. One domain in particular that I have always found fascinating was the study of biology, life processes, and evolution. As it happens, some time ago in Vienna I had the pleasure of meeting one of the directors of the Max Planck Institute. He recently received the Nobel Prize for the discovery of cyclical processes, the so-called hypercycles, which explain the evolution and autocomplexification of life processes.

I could not help reflecting that, to all appearances, it looked like he has finally explained the mystery of the black box called biogenesis. Only later, however, I realized that even if it became possible to recreate such hypercycles in laboratory, it would not necessarily amount to the production of synthetic life. As a matter of fact, it turns out that the stage often assumed to be the starting point in the evolution of life is, in reality, already very advanced. And no one can explain how this stage was reached in the first place, despite a multitude of hypotheses that cut across the entire spectrum of plausibility and peculiarity. The important point is that when we look back, trying to find the so-called first cause, we are in effect back to our problem of a biogenetic black box which we don't know how to open.

For my part, I played it sly when in 1982 I sat down in Berlin to write *Biblioteka XXI wieku* (*One Human Minute*). This book consists of three parts, of which the last, "The World as Cataclysm," hypothesizes on why the giant reptiles became extinct in the Mesozoic. In my account I mentioned only briefly that the world had been created in a Big Bang; that is, I simply adopted as given the universally accepted hypothesis on the subject. However, on the last page I added a few sentences to the effect that I did not think this was necessarily the end to cosmological hypotheses. I said that there would probably be others, and that the apparent completeness of our knowledge, which seems so incontrovertible at any given time, would be in the future a subject of intense questioning. In fact, this has already come about, since all orthodox cosmological models are undergoing today a phase of careful reexamination.

In my story I said that, even if we were ever to achieve ultimate and perfect knowledge in any domain of inquiry, we would have no means of proving this. In other words, we would be unable to provide evidence that we already know all there is to be known, and that there is nothing left to be learned. If all you are trying to do is bake a cake, any good housewife will give you the recipe, and with eggs, yeast, flour, and butter you will accomplish exactly what you want. But if, instead, you want to investigate ultimate secrets of existence, the eschatological nature of the world, the genesis of mankind, and so on—this is a completely different proposition. Suddenly mysteries and enigmas start to abound. Take the AIDS virus—we have no idea where and how it originated. I even asked some professors of virology whether they could have anticipated the possibility of something like that happening. The answer was an emphatic no.

There are phenomena which appear to us mysterious and inexplicable. If you toss a coin, obviously the probability of getting heads is 50 percent. But to take a huge bucket full of coins, toss them up in the air, and have all of them come up heads—everyone will tell you that it is impossible. Either the coins had been rigged up to show heads on both sides, or there must have been some mysterious, unknown mechanism at work. And off we go in search of the mechanism. If you look at my works, the search for unknown mysterious mechanisms is a predominant part of what I write about. In general, both my fiction and nonfiction suggest that we can indeed travel quite far on the road to knowledge, but that in place of the questions for which we find answers, others, like flowers, will spring up along the way. And this is the way it is always going to be.

I remember a book I read way back when I was a young research assistant; I think the title was something like *Science's Endless Horizon*. It described essentially the same thing in terms of looking for the horizon line—the closer you get to it, the further it recedes. This metaphor mirrors in some way the essence of the search for knowledge. Naturally, there are other situations that fit into this model, for example, the assassination of John F. Kennedy. Everyone knows what happened in Dallas but, like so many other people, I cannot bring myself to believe that Oswald was working alone. On the other hand, it turned out that the truth of the matter was buried too deeply to be brought to light. Really crazy, isn't it? Such unexplained and inexplicable phenomena have always exerted a particularly strong fascination on me, the more so that the world is full of them. And literature that aspires to model the world and its complexity has an obligation to recognize this, and must not pretend that all things work as they do in the classical detective novel, where the sleuth always ends up knowing everything.

Over the years I have had to deal with many suggestions from readers who tell me how to rewrite or expand my novels. Personally I always felt that anything of such a nature would be spurious. I have accomplished my task, created a solid piece of work, and any further additions or complications would be unwarranted. I am not Alexandre Dumas who wrote *The Three Musketeers* and then happily followed it with *Twenty Years After.*

Let me give you a concrete example. When our dog died of old age, we could not bring ourselves to have another of the same breed. In strictly rational terms this is probably quite difficult to explain, and yet a living being is something else than a broken glass that can be simply replaced with another. Now, a literary work is also a kind of living whole which should not be tampered with. In my career I have received many intemperate letters from my readers, especially on the subject of *The Investigation*, all of them in no vague terms demanding an explanation. They were particularly incensed about the lack of solution to the mystery, demanding to be told how it was possible that the corpses should move, and so on. A propos

Solaris: once I even got a letter from a Russian ex-psychiatrist, in which she wrote a continuation of my novel, since I would not even hear about doing anything like that myself. I just put this thing away, onto a big pile of other such "contributions." This is my readers' creative output; aroused by what in their view is the inadequacy of some of my books' endings, they write out further adventures, asking me to accept them as my own, or, in some cases, even to continue their labors.

I regard *Solaris* as a modeling whole which need not be extended past the frame of its narrative thought-experiment. You remember the argument between Bohr and Einstein. Einstein was on the side of determinism, and Bohr on the side of indeterminism in their interpretation of quantum mechanics (as well as the whole universe). In the category of human experience, that is, normal human common sense, the fact that the momentum and location of a particle do not exist until they are measured, that they are only virtual, or that the particle is at once a particle and a wave—this is simply inconceivable. One cannot honestly claim to understand it—I do not mean, of course, in the sense of writing a Schrödinger equation for it, but in the same sense that one understands what it means to kick a football.

Of course, subsequent experiments proved Einstein wrong and entrenched the indeterminism implicit in Heisenberg's uncertainty principle. Still, there were those who argued for the existence of the so-called hidden variables, even after von Neumann constructed his famous proof to show that no hidden variables existed. All the same, the battle was lost by the determinists of the Einsteinian school; they had to come to terms with the fact that the world is constructed in a way that is impossible for the human mind to conceive to the last detail. Once I used the following metaphor: mathematics is the white cane in the hand of a blind man. Even without fully understanding the world of quanta, just like the blind man who uses the cane to feel his way, we feel our way toward the atom bomb or the laser. And when these are constructed and made to work, we can see that our mathematical cane must have been effective, since it led us to a given application.

Swirski: *What you are saying is that the whole of mathematics—in fact the whole of science—is a kind of black box, considering that we can never know to the last detail why things happen the way they do?*

Lem: Absolutely. Jacob Bronowski described it once very nicely. He said that in science one is allowed to ask only how something works, but not what it is. Consider gravity: there are Newton's equations, there is Einstein's continuum, but what gravity really is, we are not allowed to ask. In general, in the natural sciences one is not interested in asking questions about the essence of things, because it does not get you anywhere. Clearly, pushing a physicist around until he makes up his mind and tells you whether the electron is a particle or a wave, or beating him up, no matter how badly, won't change the fact that there is no answer to this question. Thus I do not think that it is possible to find ultimate truths in the domains in which we look for them. There are no ultimate truths, period.

If we take *Solaris* as a concrete example, I still insist that the novel is well constructed because it—more precisely the library scene—clearly suggests the existence of an enormous body of professional literature on the subject of the planet and the ocean. The entire action of the novel is, in a certain sense, almost like an aftershock. The book describes the twilight phase, the decadence of solaristics; there had been ten thousand hypotheses, and they all came to nothing.

Swirski: *Given all this past industry, it is all the more surprising that nobody has tried to utilize the enormous powers of the solaristic ocean.*

Lem: What you are saying is very much to the point. The Earth is twelve thousand kilometers in diameter. Take a very big apple of a diameter of twelve centimeters, which will make it the equivalent of a scale of 1:10,000,000. The Earth's crust, that is, its lithosphere—the hard shell on which we live—is more or less equivalent in thickness to the skin on the apple; all the rest is the other "spheres," buried underneath. Theoretically the extraction of the so-called thermal energy on an industrial scale is quite possible: you simply dig a hole, fit a pipe, boil the water, and carry away the steam. Iceland utilizes to some extent the power of its geysers. But, in practice, nothing can be done on a really large scale because, if you stick a pipe deep in there, it is simply going to melt. The most you will produce is something akin to a volcanic eruption, and quite a dangerous one too.

Next to the forces contained inside our own planet, under this thin tenuous rock shell, human beings are completely helpless. So the answer to your question, "Why don't the scientists utilize the technology of the solaristic ocean?" is very simple: because they are powerless and incapable of prevailing over it. They simply cannot harness the immense energy contained in the ocean. And if I had assumed that they could—because as a writer I am free to do something like that—I would have felt as if I had sinned against the holy spirit of science.

I have always been very mindful of data coming from the sciences. I have long been a member of Carl Sagan's Conference on Extra-Terrestrial Intelligence (CETI), the commission devoted to the study of, and later also the search for, extraterrestrial civilizations. One characteristic point about their analyses has been that, over the years, they continuously had to magnify the putative distances among cosmic civilizations, increasing them first to tens and later to thousands of light years. And still we cannot find anybody out there. The enigma is growing bigger and bigger. But in literary fiction nobody pays heed to these facts; there, cosmic civilizations are always as numerous as flies in summer. To sum up: when the author decides to hypothesize beyond the certainty of contemporary knowledge, he ought to keep his material and his imagination in check not only by minding the best of available data on the subject, but also his aesthetic sense.

Swirski: *In* Summa *you discuss the point known from sociology that a society could optimize its functioning by disindividualizing the social structure of its institutions. In other words, it should be to the benefit of the society, as a hierarchically superior organism, to turn individuals into replaceable elements of the social "machine." Yet creative dynamism often goes hand in hand with exceptionality, with people who do not fit into a uniform mold. Can we sacrifice uniqueness and individuality—both in the arts and the sciences—at the altar of functional efficiency? On the other hand, individuality in art is a persistent romantic myth; the aim of an artist is precisely to "entice" the society to think and experience in terms of his creation. Artistic novelty often leads to a cult following which precisely robs the participating/spectating individuals of their personal input into the culture.*

Lem: Let me summarize all this with the following concept: anthood. An ant community is invulnerable, to a much larger degree than any other, to all forms of individualistic anarchy. In human terms Japan might be a good example. After the United States, Japan is second in per capita national income, and its monstrous export capabilities have become a serious threat today both to Europe and America. The Japanese achieve such extraordinary results because, in relative terms, their work is cheaper than that in the United States. Rich nations, to put it colloquially, grow fat, becoming more and more comfort-minded. The Germans, for example, have no longer such zest for work as they did even forty years ago (which explains their perceived feeling of being under threat). In terms of what I have just said, one might be tempted to say that the Germans have become less antlike. These days they are no longer so preoccupied with work and development; there is a feeling of wanting to spend the earned income, of enjoying the luxuries that life has to offer—in other words, a bit of hedonism. In contrast, Japanese civilization is much less indulgent in this respect. However, when all is considered, this is not a matter which can be decided by an appeal to a simple monodimensional analysis.

The developments of the recent years indicate that even Americans are losing their edge. You can hear all across the United States cries of dismay, deploring the deteriorating quality of American secondary and postsecondary education. On the other hand, the Japanese have made immense strides in this area. I am well acquainted with this situation since my son has been studying physics in the States. As long as I did not have any firsthand information, American universities seemed a bit like genius farms. Now I am beginning to realize that these places are simply full of snobs. Here we can observe the early stages of a process that could probably be identified as decadence. A problem of another dimension is that, although Nobel Prizes are still awarded to individuals, the time of the bishops in the church of science has passed. Contemporary research is conducted by massive agglomerations of people and, as a consequence, for every Nobel Prize laureate there are a thousand collaborators.

Swirski: *You state that science ought to examine "everything that we can at all examine" (Summa 110) since many important discoveries may otherwise escape our notice. Yet the number of relations between everything is infinite, and science could never get anywhere in the face of an infinity of variables and relations. If Derek de Solla Price was right in* Little Science: Big Science,[2] *we will always need selectors and filters in the way of research priorities, theoretical implications, current needs, and so on. I understand that scientists should make every effort to explore all scientific nooks and crannies for fear of overlooking*

important discoveries. But examining everything that we can at all examine?
This sounds like an impossibility from the start.

Lem: Not quite. A situation where we look for some x (it could be, for example, the number of bacteria in a patient's organism), because we do not know whether x exists, is qualitatively different from a situation where we hypothesize that x could be found, if only we could examine other phenomena but there are not enough people to do the job. Here we come back to the source you have just mentioned and its notorious futurological projection (which, in the meantime, has become much less notorious, because true). The more pessimistic of scientific estimates, which had extrapolated from the quantity of professional scientific literature appearing in all disciplines, indicated that shortly after the year 2000 the numbers for every discipline should be approaching infinity—an obviously impossible situation. I have been involved in numerous discussions on that subject at the Moscow Academy of Sciences, at the time when Soviet science was still strong. The results of these extrapolations presented a picture of the world in 2020 where every living person, no matter what sex or age, would have to be a scientist in some discipline or another. One corollary of this picture was, of course, that after 2020 humanity would simply run out of people, even if it wanted just to keep up with this acceleration of research demand.

The informational deluge in the scientific—and humanistic—disciplines is a very real and palpable problem. I have often compared myself to a man who, although himself not actively participating in scientific research, still tries to keep up with it. He finds himself in the situation of a passenger who not only faces the specter of the train leaving the station without him, but must choose from a vast number of trains, all of which are taking off in different directions. The very fact that I have in my study a pile of unread journals is a sure sign that I have already exceeded the quantitative threshold of information that I can digest.

How are we supposed to analyze all this? To begin, we can use computers, expert systems, and the like. Mind you, they can be quite inefficient; they are like a coarse sieve, which many important things may slip through. We would still have to select and choose among whatever it is that they might be analyzing for us. This is even more true in the domains that are currently undergoing rapid growth and expansion. Take genetics, for example. The pace of proliferation and diversification in genetic research is so horrific that the field, still relatively homogeneous not so long ago, now has branched out beyond belief. The same with mathematics: the theory of probability has split up into various subdomains. People working in analysis have problems communicating with their colleagues in algebra because even their jargons have become to some degree incompatible. People just have to come to terms with their finitude and mortality. On top of everything, all efforts to contain this avalanche of information run in parallel with strong evidence that the quantity of false information produced by fraudulent researchers is equally on the increase. There is no mystery behind it: it is on the increase in the same way that the quantity of counterfeit money grows together with the general quantity of money in circulation.

All the same I think that in some areas computers should indeed be able to help. It is estimated that 10, perhaps even 15 percent of all research is undertaken because it is going to be less costly than conducting a search across the professional literature of the entire world to establish whether someone else has already done a given study before. Fraud in science is facilitated today by the fact that the key individuals—for example, directors, scientific councils, Nobel Prize winners—are no longer capable of verifying whether all data is genuine, whether it may have been tampered with or falsified. To prevent this, one would have to assign a controller to each and every researcher—but that would create a form of scientific police.

Recently there was a giant uproar in the press over an American junior researcher who reported the fraudulent practices of her superiors. She lost her job because of that and for two years could not find another. And all this bogus data was okayed by a Nobel Prize recipient, David Baltimore! Still, this was just a chance discovery, the tip of the iceberg. Paradoxically almost, the situation is a little different in Poland. Because Polish science has no money and no fancy equipment, scientific fraud is relatively negligible. Still, the quality of science and, even more generally, research in Poland is constantly deteriorating. This is one phenomenon that cuts across disciplinary divides between the sciences and the humanities. I am aware, for instance, that large numbers of people from the humanities, and especially from literary studies, are desperately trying to retrain themselves for one reason only: they cannot earn enough to survive.

Here we are moving already beyond the world of science and into the domain of social phenomena typical of contemporary civilizations. Also, we must not forget the presence of the phenomena of mass culture and mass consumption, both in science and in the arts. Moreover, the products of scientific research are of a utilitarian nature, that is, they often give rise to applied technology, like various kinds of weapon systems, food products, drugs, and so on. And the control of all this is also an immense undertaking. The world is clearly becoming more and more complicated, and it is an irreversible process.

When I wrote in *Summa* about studying everything, I was not speaking in terms of what should, but of what could be done. There are things that could be done but which nobody is interested in doing. There are problems which science regards in the most fundamental sense as fictional and sterile, for example, the matter of UFOs or telepathy. No scientist worthy of the name is eager to pursue these subjects since it would obviously be a waste of time. For myself I even invented a name for these centrifugal, marginal epiphenomena; I call them the "halo effect," shimmering around the center of science. Some thirty years ago I even wrote a long article on the subject of paranormal phenomena, arguing that thirty years down the road nothing would change in this domain. Thirty years have elapsed, and we continue to be told that the real breakthrough is just around the corner, that soon we will understand and master these phenomena technologically. That's baloney; such promises are just a lot of hot air for the sake of the media.

Our civilization is menaced by the AIDS virus, but what is even worse is that we do not know what other viruses might yet attack in the future. There is a cattle virus from England, the mad cow disease—completely inexplicable. When things like that begin to happen, humanity must— like a country attacked by an enemy army—mobilize its own armies of scientists.

To say that we should examine everything means only that we should not research exclusively those areas that have a direct and predictable utility. This is a typical kind of behavior, especially in the United States. It is ubiquitous; witness the recent de facto suspension of further exploration of the moon, Mars, and outer space. Both houses of Congress determinedly refuse to fund these programs. It is kind of strange, since there is so much valuable research involved in the space program, and even more so considering Kennedy's spectacular success. If in less than ten years he put the Americans on the moon, people could be walking on Mars in fifteen if only proper funding could be secured. Still, I am not sure that I would be happy with such allocation of funds. The project would cost at least fifteen billion dollars in real terms. Considering the nightmarish state in which our planet is today, the contamination of the atmosphere, soil, and water, it looks like we cannot really afford this kind of investment.

Going back to *Summa:* despite everything I said, it is not a book that I necessarily regard as a kind of bible. Not every word in it should be taken as sacred. Quite the contrary—I myself even wrote an essay to that effect called "Thirty Years Later." The entire article is devoted to the examination of an important section of *Summa,* devoted to the subject of virtual reality, from the perspective of thirty years' progress. I even wrote there that I would gladly publish a new critical edition of *Summa,* much enlarged to include—in the margins, footnotes, or in some other way—my commentary on the things I wrote in the 1960s. My aim in this hypothetic reedition would be to evaluate what has in the meantime come true, what has not, and which of my hypotheses are in need of correction in light of new knowledge.

As for studying everything that is at all possible to study—at times our inability to do that can be actually to our advantage. During Hitler's times, not only for financial and technological reasons but also owing to the intellectual limitations of Hitler and his associates, German physicists did not examine everything that they could have and did not initiate full-scale research into the atomic bomb. Symptomatically, they failed to pursue this line of research because their government saw all science in terms of an immediate utility of results. In another totalitarian camp, when the Soviet authorities demanded immediate utility of research, they immediately got their results in the person of Trofim Lysenko. For Lysenko heredity in plants (but also heredity in general) was a kind of unruly phenomenon that could be bullied this way or that to suit our preferences. The results of this idiocy were, of course, immense losses in Soviet agriculture and related disciplines, running into billions and billions of dollars.

To sum it up: all I was saying in *Summa* is that basic research should be conducted independently of our perception of whether it is going to bring tangible profits by tomorrow. It is never totally clear what will be of most use to us in the future. We move in the darkness of our ignorance, and must never forget that some of our most important discoveries, like the laser or penicillin, were completely accidental. My guiding thought was that we must not confine ourselves to narrow forms of utilitarianism, especially given that we are surrounded by massive market pressures, regulated only by the desire to maximize marketability and profit. Hence all these new car models which are not always better than the old ones but which are produced anyway, just because people have been trained to believe that a car *modo anno* 1998 is certainly superior to the model from 1997.

The same obtains for books. I first noticed it in Germany, where my editors can take *The Cyberiad,* divide it in half, wrap the halves in new covers, paste on new titles, and send them off to the bookstore. Apparently the sales are better this way. That's the exactly same thing as with automobiles, a chronic inflation of value. On the other hand, market-driven editors fail to take into account other things, such as, for example, that the philosophy of Hume or Kant has not aged since it was written. The sole trend they see is this planned obsolescence of all products, which for them includes the products of human thought as well. Sad, but true.

Swirski: *With the exception of* The Magellan Nebula, *and maybe a couple of other novels scattered over the decades, there are no significant female characters in your fictions. Why this prominent absence, especially in light of your commitment to social and psychological realism?*

Lem: I think there were actually a number of reasons, some of which I am perhaps not completely aware. I do not doubt for a moment that the author is not always the best expert on the reasons—sometimes only semi-deliberate—behind a given selection of characters. I must say that I am actually quite attached to some of the female characters from my works. To take a concrete example, in *Hospital of the Transfiguration* there is Doctor Wasilewska, whom Bereś (a Polish critic) characterized rather nastily as sexually frigid. He wrote that because nothing explicitly erotic happens in the novel. But I regarded it as unnecessary. Anyway, why the absence of women? I think there were several reasons. Let me start with the most recent.

I am terribly irritated by the contemporary injunction in North America that when one writes about someone, say a physicist, it has to be in the form "he or she." I am thoroughly opposed to this, and when they requested my permission to use this convention in the American translations, I categorically refused. I told them that they could print my texts, but only as they were. This is the same kind of absurdity as referring to God as a "she"— a peculiar concept, considering that he is male in all monotheistic religions. I don't see a reason for changing this; I did not start the convention, nor am I going to change it to suit some people. Furthermore, if we consider the statistics, the number of female geniuses is certainly nowhere near the number of males; there is a preponderance here (naturally, there are significant exceptions).

Another reason is that the introduction of women is for me an unnecessary complication, if I can be excused for speaking so cynically about my fictions. In other words, to bring women on board a spaceship—I am speaking of course in a terribly simplified way—and not draw from this any narrative conclusions, whether sexual, erotic, emotional, or any other, would be a form of falsehood. It would not make sense to have the crew stay in isolation, like two convents, one male, the other female, would it? But if I have a certain narrative and cognitive design to execute, then an introduction of women can be inconvenient, and even contrary to my plan, even if only by requiring complexification.

On the other hand, in novels like *Solaris*, the heroine duplicated by the ocean is necessary, since the ocean itself is such a complexifying factor in a certain sense. In other words, I work according to a functional principle: if I need a female character then I will introduce one. It is not a coincidence that the monstrous heroine of "The Mask" is a woman of wondrous beauty who is, in fact, a kind of basilisk, monster, demon, embodied in an automated machine. This was necessitated by the demands of the plot. So the presence of women in my stories is in each case determined by specific narrative requirements.

Swirski: *You wrote extensively on virtual reality in* Summa, *but I would like to discuss it in the example of a story from* Tales of Pirx the Pilot. *At the beginning, when still a cadet, Pirx takes his exams, as a part of which he pilots a small rocket to the moon. On the way he is involved in a near-fatal crash—then suddenly the lights come on, he is back at the exam center, it's been all phantomatics—a virtual-reality experience.*

Lem: That's right, this is all a part of the test.

Swirski: *In* Summa *you analyzed the problem of distinguishing between reality and phantomatized illusion. You wrote about several uncomplicated parameters—perspiration, tiredness, hunger, and so on—which could be used by the subject to determine his state. However, in the Pirx story, in the phantomatic* *state the protagonist experiences accelerations of several g's. It would appear that with such a sophistication of the virtual-reality machinery the tests which you mention in* Summa *would be insufficient to determine the state of the subject, thus reopening the specter of synthetic prison-realities. How do you view this problem today?*

Lem: Virtual reality (VR) is a technology already in use, available to anyone who can afford the expense. Everywhere you go you can find catalogs listing equipment and prices. The greatest difficulty at the present time is not even excessive gravity, which could be created by means of a centrifuge, like those used in astronaut training centers. The toughest challenge would be to achieve a simulation of weightlessness. This is one thing which we could not achieve in any other way than in free fall, but it would be difficult (if not impossible) to dress some fellow in a special sensorized suit and throw him down from a great height, so that he could experience free fall—not to say anything about taking him up into orbit. To generalize, there are situations which occur in the real world that at the present moment we are not capable of transforming into a phantomatic experience, with the understanding, of course, that we can never exclude the possibility that future changes and improvements may allow it.

In "Thirty Years Later" I set out to compare my own prognoses from the 1960s—when the subject of virtual reality was still unmitigated fantasy—with what has already been realized today. My main focus was philosophical and sociological; I was thus writing of ontological limitations of VR machines, of things which as a society we cannot do, and so on. On the other hand, I heard that Simon and Schuster recently offered $75,000 to a computer programmer who is supposed to write about having sex with a computer in the context of virtual reality. In my study I wrote that such future erotic trends are, of course, possible; however, I also said that it would be not only much more difficult but also more interesting to arrange a chat with somebody like Einstein.

To construct a phantomatic imitation of sexual intercourse is really to engineer a form of onanism, which is much easier to achieve than to create a program with sufficient intellectual powers to think and discourse like Einstein. This feat lies still maybe a hundred years in the future, even though I would not want to commit myself here to any specific dates, since predictions are really difficult to make in this area. Anyway, it is clear that the degree of difficulty is quite different in either case. Sex with computers in virtual reality is, no doubt, possible. But, when discussing phantomatics in *Summa*, I was, as a matter of principle, more interested in the phantomatic consequences of the old Berkeleyan motto, *Esse est percipi* (To be is to be perceived), and in VR as the first stage of technological invasion into the domain of concepts of purely philosophical nature.

Swirski: *In* The Futurological Congress *you play with the idea of irreality, with the idea of an endless regression of multiple layers of synthetic reality. You refrain from a neuro-cybernetic description of this "world within a world" effect and use a pharmacological one instead. Is this model plausible, considering that the human brain is built of cells that morphologically are very similar to one another? The pharmacological technology as you describe it would have to have a fantastic selectivity to do the job you ask it to do.*

Lem: Your question is really a question about literary, and specifically narrative, conventions. When you write a futurological novel, you can always set up the limiting parameters as you please. In my fictions I always make an effort to include as little technical jargon as possible. Why introduce cybernetic terminology, get entangled in specific terms, complications, and such, when you can "invent" a drug which causes good mood, a "benignimizer" or something like that. There is, however, a completely different aspect of *The Futurological Congress* that also needs to be taken into account. As the critics began to mention in the later stages of the downfall of communism in Poland, the central theme of the novel is the very issue you have brought up: the layering of illusion and deception, the falsehood of reality that paints the depicted civilization as magnificent, whereas, in reality, it is nothing short of horrid.

On this interpretation, my novel is about a game devised by the Orwellian Polish government, which tried to persuade us that, while we lived in affluence and happiness, the West wallowed in penury. In Poland it was always difficult to find converts to this creed, but many citizens of the Soviet Union believed it for a long time. Indeed, this is the very nature of the psychemical world I described in *The Futurological Congress,* only the role performed in our real world by ordinary lying propaganda was played in the novel by psychemical technologies. So, in a sense, this particular virtual-reality solution is also a metaphor that should not always be taken literally. I will give you another example: when I wrote my first novel, *The Astronauts,* one renowned physicist wrote to me that with the parameters of power and thrust which I gave the rocket, it could never fly to Venus. I wrote him back then—although I have stopped getting involved in this kind of thing since—that if I were really a designer of rockets which could fly to Venus, then I would not write novels but design spaceships instead.

Swirski: *Could you comment on the philosophical or even metaphysical beliefs underlying your work?*

Lem: My philosophy, or rather my philosophical views, are neither coherent nor very systematic; that is to say I do not subscribe to any single school of philosophy unconditionally. In a sense, in the face of these different schools and systems, I am a kind of wide-ranging heretic. I do not write in order to popularize certain philosophical concepts, simply because I do not think about them at all when I write.

Everyone knows that, for all their phenomenal processing power, computers do not understand anything, whereas even a small child understands very well the meaning of a sneeze, because the book the child just lifted from the shelf was covered with dust. This kind of knowledge is available to children almost prelinguistically, being further developed as a result of relevant experience. Nothing like that can happen to the computer since the machine is not capable of amassing experience, being thus, in comparison with children, completely stupid. In an analogical way, my whole philosophical stance when I write fiction is also completely instinctive (I am speaking here exclusively of my fictions, and not essays or nonfictional studies like *Summa*).

In the human activities of the rational, instrumental, technological, mercantile, or medicinal kind, the highest court of appeal is always a given collection of professional information that every specialist must defer to. An honest doctor will not treat cancer with toothpaste because he knows that it does not make sense. On the other hand, the highest court of appeal to which we defer in order to establish sense and coherence in a literary work is not just available data about the real world, but rather the genre paradigm. Thus in a novel written by a Catholic writer, his characters can see the Virgin Mary or a saint performing a miracle, in a way that need not be a hallucination or an illusion. Similarly, if you write a novel about a clairvoyant who really and truly sees the future, no one can censure you for this just because they believe soothsaying does not exist. This type of freedom cuts across all fiction. Nobody gets incensed with a fairy-tale writer because he has created a witch who, when she casts a comb to the ground, makes a dense forest spring up. The paradigmatic structure of the fairy tale allows the writer to do that, as well as a whole lot of other things.

In the same way, when I write my fictions, I can approach certain issues conventionally. I can pretend, for example, that I do not realize that *Solaris* depicts a solar system situated very far away from Earth. We all know that if it was really that far, nobody could reach it in the span of human life without some form of hibernation or other technology. I am perfectly well aware of that, but I leave all this, as it were, outside the covers of the book. The reason, if I can put it this way, is simply because it would be awkward for me to get into my bed of creation wearing heavy boots of realism. *Solaris* is about love and the mysterious ocean, and that is what is important about it. As to how the protagonist actually got to the planet, I pretend that I do not know.

For literature the highest court of appeal, the tribunal of rights and faults, is literature itself. It is as if you were to ask a poet why he bothers to rhyme his lines instead of writing in blank or free verse. The question makes no sense next to the simple fact that such is the literary paradigm chosen by the poet. *Licentia poetica* sanctions certain violations of truths known to us from reality. Such violations should, of course, be well justified. If I assume certain things for the sake of writing a novel—for example, something which seems physically impossible—there ought to be very compelling reasons for such a move, which should become evident in the course of reading. Put simply, people work for profit; if someone forges currency, he does it for profit, and not for the sake of keeping counterfeit money in his drawer.

Swirski: *You have often maintained that even contemporary science, which employs terms and symbols that have no referents available to our immediate sensorium, describes something real that lies behind these symbols. This is ultimately a form of scientific realism. On the most basic level, this would involve a belief in a palpable, external reality, in contrast to social solipsism which claims that we all define and create reality via our socio-cultural existence.*

Lem: Yes it does. It is extraordinarily funny, but one argument against solipsism which I find especially persuasive goes back to the great Bertrand

Russell. Logically, of course, one cannot prove anything in this matter. We can neither prove that solipsism is false, nor, for that matter, disprove that the world was created only seconds ago, together with human beings who had everything preprogrammed in their heads in such a way that subjectively they feel as if everything had been there before: the world, themselves, and history.

Russell's thought experiment went like this: Imagine I walk up to a shelf in my library, take out the sonnets by Shakespeare, and read them. If my solipsistic belief is to be consistent, I must conclude that there never was any Shakespeare, and that these lyrics are a creation of my own brain. At this point I have to reflect (continues Russell) that as Russell I could never write sonnets as good as the ones I have read. This leads me to conclude that there probably did exist a man called Shakespeare, who wrote much better poetry than I. There is nothing, of course, to prevent me from expanding my point of view, so, looking at this enormous library, I reflect again: "Here are all these books, each one about things of which I had no idea. And all of this is to be the creation of nothing else but my brain?" Russell's account is, of course, not a bona fide logical argument but, as a commonsensical analysis of solipsism, it is extremely powerful and credible.

On the other hand, it does not make much sense to look for answers to questions of the sort, "What does a room look like when there is no one around to see it?" I see this problem in the following way: if there were a fly in the room, we might be able to photograph the room through its eyes and see how the fly saw the room. If instead of a fly there were a dog, we could presumably do the same. But to ask whether, in the absence of anybody to see it, the room is a collection of atoms or a collection of objects, does not make sense. Everything depends on the scale of perception. We are made the way we are, with hands, legs, a sense of hearing and sight, and we are made to perceive things in a certain way. If we were constructed differently then, naturally, we would perceive things in a different way. The question about the room is as senseless as asking what a star *really* is. We can say that a star is a ball of incandescent gas and proceed to enumerate its physical parameters. But if we wanted to approach it *really* close to examine it with our own eyes, the only sensible answer at this point is that we would turn into gas in the monstrous radiation and temperatures of the star.

This is of course a form of incompatibility. Our sensorium is designed to deal with objects which do not stray too far from the scale delimited by our own bodies and temperatures. If we wanted to know how our sensorium would behave in the vicinity of the temperature of 100 million degrees, which is the temperature accompanying the explosion of the hydrogen bomb, the answer is that we would turn into gas the instant of the explosion. We would not perceive anything; our scale of perception is inherently limited, whether we like it or not. In other words, the world exists independently of whether it is inhabited by mankind or not.

In *Summa* I dealt with this problem in a slightly different form. I asked about the existential status of typewriters in the Mesozoic. Clearly there were no typewriters then, but if only people had lived at that time, a typewriter could have potentially been built. There was iron ore—it was possible to build a furnace, make screwdrivers, hammers, and other tools. This is a facultative, pure possibility, but it does not contradict the fact that from a rational, commonsensical point of view all this is plausible and correct. The Earth has been around for much longer than the existence of the human species, and although we do not know how life originated, or how *Homo sapiens* separated from the hominids, we accept as highly plausible that it did somehow happen. But if there is one thing we are not ready to believe, it is that it all happened through the intervention of a sorcerer, or that we found ourselves on this planet only two weeks ago owing to a divine miracle. While remaining aware of its shortcomings, I am thus a proponent of a commonsensical approach to these matters.

These shortcomings were, nota bene, the subject of intense dissatisfaction to no less a thinker than Sir Arthur Eddington. It appeared strange to him that there seemed to have been two tables in front of him: one of the old-fashioned kind on which he rested his elbows, and the other a mere cloud of electrons. Today one does not have to limit oneself to electrons, but may consider a vacuum with its virtual particles. Besides, the table is also a microscopic chunk of energy, so it generates a certain gravitational field, no matter how immeasurably small. This is the domain of the physics of the twentieth century, but if we went back to Aristotle, he would see the whole thing quite differently, since he did not know anything about atoms or electrons. As Russell put it, reality is given to us in a way that we perceive by means of our senses; everything else is the product of our hypotheses and reasoning.

My attitude to philosophy in general? There are philosophers whom I like, even though I do not necessarily agree with everything they have to say. I feel a great amount of affinity and respect for Schopenhauer, even though his whole system of the world as Will and Imagination leaves me quite underwhelmed. I like Bertrand Russell very much for his skeptical and sober attitude. This is a typically English brand of philosophy, phlegmatic and analytic to the core. In contrast, I completely cannot stand the phenomenologists, Heidegger, Husserl, and especially this lunatic Derrida and his neoscholastic theorizing. I cannot deny the contribution and sensibility of Popper and his school of thinking; falsifiability is a useful notion, and Popper himself was an astute thinker. But then from the master's shadow sprang the student, Paul Feyerabend, an apostate and a heretic of the entire Popperian school. I even contested Feyerabend on the pages of some German journal, although I refrained from calling him too many names, whereas he really let himself go. The heart of the matter was his claim that scientific induction and all other forms of scientific reasoning do not necessarily lead to the truth, and that all methods which yield testable results are equally good. I am essentially not opposed to what he was saying, but I had to take a stand when he started going too far, propounding some sort of anarchic dadaism as a theory of cognition.

In matters of philosophy and philosophy of science my attitude is a bit like Gombrowicz's in his *Diary*.[3] It is quite droll, his vision of these many smelting furnaces, white with heat, and the strolling figure of the author who says to himself, "Here is a piece of a Heideggerian concept, let's take a bite and see how it tastes." So he does, and says, "Too hot and too bitter for my taste," after which he walks over to the place where Sartre sits and thinks of nothingness and void, but again departs after a brief stay, saying, "I don't like this taste either; too depressing." Existential nothingness is really too sad and depressing for me—you could almost say that I do not like the way it tastes. I must confess that my attitude toward particular philosophical systems is not devoid of an extra dimension, which makes me accept them not only because they are credible and plausible, but also because they appeal to me in an aesthetic sense.

In scientific, as well as metascientific (i.e., philosophical) research the aesthetic quality of the analytic shape in which a theory can be expressed is one of the factors codetermining its acceptance. I think this factor is at the bottom of the rather mysterious and somewhat inexplicable affinity between musical and mathematical creations. My son, for example, in contrast to me, is very talented musically. He composes music, plays a number of instruments, even though he is principally interested in physics and mathematics. My own relation to music is altogether different. For me the process ended with Beethoven; to Bach I could not warm up too much, and there is nothing I can do about it. For that matter, I totally adore Chopin, but cannot tolerate atonal music—Stravinsky means absolutely nothing to me. I prefer Beethoven's Fifth Symphony to the Seventh, and the Ninth induces in me a state of wild ecstasy. And I am not even sure that I could articulate why it should be so.

My attitude to various philosophical systems is essentially no different. I am irritated by Sartre and his thousand-page ponderosities. Popper makes a lot of sense in what he writes; on the other hand, he is too much like a schoolteacher, wagging his finger ex cathedra while proclaiming that things are such and such, and you cannot disagree with him at the risk of being taken by the ear and thrown out of the classroom. Then there are philosophers like Husserl, or better still Wittgenstein, who in the first half of his life wrote *Tractatus Logico-Philosophicus* (1922), and later denied everything he had written in *Philosophical Investigations* (1953). Excuse me, but to study someone who fights battles with himself could be of interest only to people who have more time to spare than myself.

But all this writing does not even graze the surface of the difficulties and dilemmas with which philosophers must contemporarily come to terms. What, for example, is one supposed to do with the fact that the same mathematical structure of a law (or theory) of physics may give rise to totally different, or even incompatible, interpretations? Scientists try to explain what it means for the same entity to be sometimes matter and at other times a wave, but it does not change the fact that this duality can be interpreted in a number of ways. At the same time, one *must* accept theories which, strange as they may sometimes sound, have been confirmed experimentally.

I must confess that in the domain of philosophy I consider myself to be a layman since I never studied it in a systematic way. Why? Wittgenstein wrote once that many of the problems posed by physics only appear as such because of the bottleneck formed by our language. For this reason he did not consider them to be real problems but only apparent ones (I suppose one consequence of that is the subsequent popularity of philosophy of language). For my part, I think that the world of knowledge is incomparably greater than Wittgenstein ever imagined. It dwarfs any individual by the immensity of the intellectual vistas that open up on an almost daily basis. A polymath, a multispecialist educated in many different disciplines, may have a slightly better grasp of the present state of inquiry; on the other hand, there is nobody, no single human being, able to encompass all the diverse strands and domains of learning and understanding. Perhaps it might have been still possible in Plato's times, but we have left that era behind. Now everybody marches alone in the darkness, using his own little flashlight of knowledge to find the way. I am the first to admit that, out of the eight or ten thousand books in my home library, there are some several hundred that I have not even had time to glance at. And this is, after all, only a drop in the ocean which surrounds us.

Recently there has been a proliferation of hypotheses in light of which the universe is a kind of computer which, by dint of its "programming," generates nebulae, stars, and other cosmic bodies. In my opinion the proponents of these theories are really pushing it. People like Fritjof Capra are to me simple charlatans who mix metaphysics, rationality, and irrationality, making it into a kind of intellectual stir-fry designed to grab people's attention.

In Conan Doyle's "The Hound of the Baskervilles" there is a single risky path which leads to the center of the swamp where the dog is kept. If one did not know the way, it was very easy to be led astray and drown in the swamp. As a civilization, we are in a similar predicament today. We must find a way amid the overwhelming immensity of scientific and nonscientific information, so that we do not end up drowning in it. The easiest way out, naturally, is to believe everything, no matter how outrageous or counterfactual. Let's be frank: people want to be deceived, especially when face to face with endless numbers of professional books and articles. You can almost hear them say: "Why learn about the theory of relativity, why spend months probing the arcane mysteries of quantum mechanics? I'll just read Capra and I'll know everything." Better still, as in Poland, why read anything at all, when all they need to do is go to church and listen to the priest who proclaims that God is omniscient, that one must have faith without any questions, reservations, or such like. All smart alecks, the priest might add, are led to sin more easily, thus risking the ultimate misfortune of being left outside the privileged circle of the meek and faithful.

I assume full and unmitigated responsibility for my actions, which means that I want to use my flashlight of knowledge for as long as possible. There are problems which I realize I am not competent to solve, and when I become aware of it, I ask advice of someone who knows more than I do. The conviction that one has learned all there is to learn is one of the most pernicious self-delusions that can ever befall anybody.

Swirski: *Your last thoughts on literature and philosophy?*

Lem: My last thoughts? I am a staunch adherent to the maxim that literature, much as philosophy, should never bore its readers to death. Reading should never be a matter of struggling through a jungle of words and concepts, with difficulty and discomfort, in order to grasp what should come naturally. All things considered, I also respect thinkers of courage. I do not know whether it qualifies as a courageous act, but one reason that I like Russell so much was that he had the intellectual and moral integrity to call Hegel—without pulling any punches—a complete idiot. I totally concur: Hegel is an idiot, and those who praised his work have only been doing themselves a great disservice. Intellectual honesty and humility—this is what we all need.

Edited and translated by Peter Swirski

Notes

1. R. Duncan Luce and Howard Raiffa, *Games and Decisions: Introduction and Critical Survey* (New York: Wiley, 1957).

2. New York: Columbia University Press, 1963.

3. Witold Gombrowicz, *Diary,* 3 vols. (Evanston, Ill.: Northwestern University Press, 1988–93; original spans the years 1953–66).

Thirty Years Later

The full history of futurology as an enterprise given to forecasting the future and aspiring to the status of science has not (as far as I know, and I know rather little) yet been written. It will be informative, as well as pathetic and amusing, for it will show how the self-proclaimed prognosticators—and there were no others—have almost always been wrong, with the exception of those under the aegis of the Club of Rome (among others), who painted the future in black colors.

The futurological boom produced a number of best-sellers, bringing money and fame to their authors as a result of (illusory) hopes entertained by both politicians and the public at large that the future *can* at last be predicted. Still, the boom turned out to be only momentary. The disappointment caused by its prognostic inaccuracy was as pathetic as the circumstances surrounding the sudden renown of leading futurologists were amusing. Suffice it to look at Herman Kahn, whose death several years ago freed him from being accountable for his predictive errors from his numerous futurological best-sellers (errors much more fundamental than either those of his acolytes or antagonists). Cofounder of the Rand Corporation and the Hudson Institute, Kahn first indulged in foretelling the horrors of a thermonuclear war; and when the winds of fashion changed, he started advancing predictions for aeons ahead (as, for example, in *The Next Two Hundred Years*). In the process he had multiplied forecasting scenarios without end, but, even though (with the aid of his staff) he had produced a stunning variety of them, nothing ever came about as predicted. Still, the above mentioned institutions have well survived both the solid fiasco of all prognoses aimed *in futurum* and the passing away of their error-prone guru, because institutions are more easily created than dissolved. The main guarantee of their longevity lies not in the success rate of their work, but their own structural rigidity. Once the millions of dollars in grants and donations had been invested, the fact that they went to waste was of no concern to those on the payroll.

It is true, though, that futurology is no longer in vogue. Although active still, it functions with much more reserve and less hubris, while its adherents and activists pursue the ironclad, or golden, rule of total amnesia. None of them ever return to their own prognoses when these founder; instead they simply write a whole bunch of new ones, and publish them with the clear conscience of hacks who do this sort of thing for a living. Such futurologists are many, but it is not my intention to expose them, for *nomina sunt odiosa*. I intend thus to write *pro domo sua*, that is, about my own modest contribution to futurology. This contribution is of double nature. Writing for over forty years now, I have become increasingly given to simple curiosity about what this world is going to look like in the future, and most of what I have written as science fiction has been guided in earnest by my inquisitive curiosity about this question. Still, no matter how correct my prognoses, once they have been advanced in the guise of literary fiction, they must no longer be regarded as part and parcel of futurological research. The reason is the *licentia poetica* which underwrites all fiction, and gives literature the right and privilege of advancing statements which lack assertion (i.e., statements which do not have to be true), but which at the same time robs them of credibility.

Maybe things will indeed happen the way they are described in a novel, and maybe they will develop completely differently. No one can blame the author, for nonassertive speculation is permissible to writers of fiction. It is for that reason that between 1961 and 1963 I tried to forsake this convenient protection from a confrontation with reality. The result was a nonbelletristic *Summa technologiae* which, however, was not completely futurological either, as this type of future writing had not then yet become popular (thus, weird as it may seem, even while writing it, I did not know well myself what exactly I was doing).[1] The book had a modest edition of three thousand copies, and essentially sank without a trace, with a single exception: Leszek Kolakowski wrote a critique of *Summa* in the November 1964 issue of *Twórczość*, under the title "Informacya i utopia" ("Information and Utopia").[2] Kolakowski wrote off the various hypotheses which constituted the prognostic essence of my book, declaring that its readers might have a hard time separating fairy tale from information. Conceding a spoonful of compliments, Kolakowski nonetheless blackened them with a barrel of tar, in his conclusion accusing me of a "liquidatory attitude" in relation to the philosophical kingdom. In particular, he singled out as highly reproachable my conjecture that in the future that very kingdom might suffer an invasion of technology. He closed off with a flourish with the following words: "So, to Merleau-Ponty's question, What has remained of philosophy in the wake of the encroachments of modern science?, one can give the same answer that he did: all that has been philosophy before."

As far as pronouncements go, this one is as unrelenting as peculiar in a philosopher who first supported Marxist philosophy against Christianity (which sought to abolish it), and later supported Christianity against Marxism. Like many others, I esteem the works of Kolakowski; perhaps most of all his *Religion,* which demonstrates from a sweeping historical perspective that the more fervently believers seek God, the sooner they bleed on the dogmas of the church, in this very manner paving the way for apostasy and sectarianism. His trilogy on Marxism interested me less simply because it is exactly as captivating as *A History of the Construction of Perpetual Motion Machines* would be. Although no such contraption can ever be constructed, for centuries men undertook the greatest labors to do just that, spawning immense numbers of original and eccentric projects. Nobody even batted an eyelid when these projects were subsequently lifted off the patient paper they were written on and pressed into construction. The same thing could be said about the theory of constructing a paradise on Earth, for which Marxism gave us—the afflicted ones—the blueprints. It also gave us, in its perennial drive toward an ever brighter future, mass graves and ruins from which it will take the greatest perseverance and difficulty to get out.

Why do I mention all this? Thirty years ago I was forced to bear in silence the critique of a philosopher who rejected all of my prognoses, for the simple reason that a prognosis is nothing but a description of states which do not yet exist. And since they do not exist, how can one defend their depiction when a distinguished thinker calls them a fairy tale in his review, and likens their author to a boy in a sandbox who, working hard with his toy spade, claims—as children are wont to do—that he is going to dig right through the Earth to the other side?

It so happens, however, that my predictions, labeled by Kolakowski as fantasies rooted in science fiction and fairy tales, have gradually be-gun to come true. For years now I have been toying with the idea of reprinting *Summa technologiae* with added commentary showing what has in the meantime come about, what is in a developmental stage, and what was aberrant in my forecasts. For now, however, I will take up only a single chapter of *Summa,* "Phantomology," for two different reasons. *Primo,* because the branch of information technology which I thought up already exists; *secundo,* because its completely nonfantastic existence did nothing to change Kolakowski's position. I understand that he did not retract his words—now so obviously unwarranted and erroneous in slamming my predictive competence—because he did not bother to read up in scientific literature on cyberspace, virtual reality, or in price catalogs which offer a rich sampling of the apparatuses which I had once imagined, now with names like Eye-Phone and Data-Glove. The reason that he did not bother is because *infallibilitas philosophica* remains the cornerstone of his attitude, and there is nothing that can happen anywhere that can challenge Kolakowski's assertive pronouncements. Such an attitude is a little odd in a philosopher whose views used to change in a zigzag fashion; I do not, however, intend to write a diatribe aimed at him, because—to repeat *verba magistri* from "Information and Utopia"—"my critique is humble."

I will recast what I had written about the encroachment of technology on the kingdom of philosophy, and juxtapose it with what has quite mundanely happened, as described *today* in specialized and learned, as well as popular, books. There are no such texts here in Poland, of course, but I do not doubt that proper translations will appear in no time at all. As a certain American said once, a precursor who appears a year or two before the big wave, wins fame and fortune. Whoever makes an entry thirty years before it, though, is at best forgotten, and at worst derided. My fate was the latter.

A discussion of one's own books does not become the author, but since nobody really tried to analyze the philosophical contents of *Summa,* I will need to summarize its subject matter, almost thirty years after its conception. The task is easier today because at the time of writing I was not even entirely sure what I was trying to accomplish. Even the overall structure eluded me at the time: I wrote the book the way "it wrote itself." Today I am able, nonetheless, to discern the reason for the rather considerable accuracy of my predictions; it is not accidental, nor does it stem from any uniquely personal talents. Quite simply, my general assumption was a conviction that life and the processes examined by the biological sciences will become an inspirational gold mine for future constructors in all phenomena amenable to the engineering approach. In this light, "breeding of information" as automated gnosis (so bizarre in the eyes of its sole critic, Kolakowski), is nothing else than a plagiarism from the natural evolution of animals and plants, since evolution *was* precisely an information breeder, aimed at the successive development of various species of all that lives from their common tree of knowledge: the genetic code. This in turn leads to the consideration of our sensory system, necessary in order to survive in the exacting environment. Consequently, the essence of the problem that underlies my chapter on phantomology (as well as the present text) is how to create realities indistinguishable from ordinary reality for the intelligent beings who live in it. "Can one," I asked in the book, "create a synthetic reality which, like a face-mask, will cover all of a person's senses, to the point where he will not be able to tell that he has been separated from the real world by means of such a 'mask/phantomatics'?"

The background to this challenge—which, as I thought, would not be accomplished until some time in the next millennium—was the doctrine of the English materialist bishop, George Berkeley. His thesis is denoted concisely by the maxim *esse est percipi*, that is, to be is to be perceived. True enough, whatever we deem as existing, owes to our perception of it, or so at least was the case during that philosopher's lifetime (1685–1753). In *A History of Western Philosophy*, a book which I prize for its originality and a calculated subjectivity of views (it characterizes Hegel as a half-wit), Bertrand Russell describes matter as whatever fulfills the parameters defined by the equations of theoretical physics.[3] The simple reason why I cannot agree with this view is that there are alternative theories in theoretical physics, and matter, if it exists (and I think so), is only one.

As an aside I must confess that, even though, out of necessity, I occasionally tried my amateur hand at philosophy, I regard its labors in a large part as sterile. The point is that there is no other way to do philosophy but by using language. (Although I had speculated on the subject of experimental philosophy, derived from philosophy of science in general and phantomology in particular, this hypothesis did not meet with much enthusiasm.) When examined in more and more detail, language paradoxically begins to look a lot like matter. When matter is examined under the magnifying lens of experiments and theories, it leads after a while to a *circulus vitiosus*, a vicious circle. What was to be the smallest, or the most elementary particle, is not so because it consists of (for example) quarks which have not even been observed—that is to say, perceived. Yet although free quarks could in theory be extracted out of matter—albeit only under monstrous pressures or temperatures—they are no longer even regarded as "tiny" building blocks of elementary particles since, strangely enough, they turn out to be somehow "big" (in the meantime no efforts are being spared to "dig" into quarks even further, in order to probe them even "deeper"). The situation is almost identical with language, where individual words are not autonomous carriers of meaning but refer instead to units of superior order. In the end it turns out that, even though language consists of words, words do not acquire meaning in any other way but from their function—from the way they are embedded—in language as a system. It is because of this messy situation, which thrusts philosophers into the debates and dilemmas of linguists, that the more a philosopher probes into the structures of statements, the more likely he is to experience the same thing as a scientist who wants to find out what a picture is made of. Supermicroscopes allow him to pass the level of magnified dots of printed ink, past the level of fluffy strings of cellulose from which paper is made, past molecules, then atoms, until he finds himself at the point where he needs to speak of quarks which, however, neither himself nor anyone else will be able to see. Put in other words, and more simply: overprecision, as a desire to reach the linguistic level of ultimate accuracy, leads into formal systems where one is engulfed by the terrible abyss discovered by Kurt Gödel. With this remark, at least for now, I must nevertheless close my digression.

By phantomatics I designated a method by means of which a person can be linked up via his entire sensorium to the computer (which I refer to as the machine or, simply, the phantomat). The computer inputs into the sensory organs, such as eyes, ears, dermis, and others, stimuli which perfectly imitate the stimuli which normally are supplied continuously by the world, that is, the ordinary environment. At the same time the computer is feedback-linked, which means that it is functionally dependent on the perceptory activity of the phantomatized person. In this way it creates an unshakable conviction in the subject of this procedure that he is in a place where he certainly is not, that he is really experiencing what is in fact only an illusion, that he is behaving in ways in which he normally never does. Such a person will experience impressions (ocular, olfactory, tactile, etc.) indistinguishable from those experienced in reality, their identicalness being here not a fantasy or an arbitrary postulate but a pivotal assumption. Thus in my phantomatic prognoses, I *assumed* that a production of stimuli indistinguishable from those which govern our senses—to wit, sight, hearing, smell—will be *possible*. In the meantime this has already happened, even though, since Rome was not built in a day, for the time being imperfections still occur. On the other hand, if the phantomat works properly, to diagnose between "I am" or "I am *not* phantomatized" turns out to be increasingly difficult and, in borderline cases, impossible. In this way Lem's fairy tale has gradually begun to turn into irrefutable fact.

Leaping right into the middle of what is already an engineering success—thus making the invasion of technology into the domain of philosophical doctrines a fact—I will quote an excerpt from an article by Paul Marx published in *New Scientist* on April 6, 1991.[4] Computer programs created by Jonathan Waldern, a specialist in the field, have compelled all those hooked up to their virtual—or, in my nomenclature, phantomatic—reality to believe so intensely that this reality was entirely authentic, that "it is an unwritten but well enforced rule at W industries that employees who have used the system must not drive a car for at least half an hour afterwards." The reason? Simply because all crashes and accidents which can be experienced in the "phantomatic session," when a person interacts with the car-driving program, naturally do not involve any dangerous consequences, so that changing from the phantomat seat to an ordinary car can easily lead to an accident.

Thus the illusion created by the computer program—which encases all senses, cutting them off from our ordinary mortal reality—makes the transfer from the synthetic to authentic existence extremely difficult. So far the above-mentioned companies have released only a limited number of programs: a simulator for airplane pilotage, space travel, flight over a designated area (e.g., over skyscrapers in downtown Seattle), as well as the already mentioned ride in a surface vehicle. All of those can be and are used in tests, in pilot training, or in driving examinations, but they will also have an incomparably wider range of applications. I will discuss them now, referring not so much to the achievements of extant technologies, but to my own thirty-year-old prognoses.

In Stanislaw Beres's *Conversations with Stanislaw Lem,* issued by Wydaw-nictwo Literackie in 1987 but written, as my interviewer relates in the preface, in 1981–82, I stated that "when I wrote about phantomatics, so interesting (if so improbable) from the point of view of experimental philosophy, I did nonetheless stress that its social consequences would probably be nightmarish" (93). The tacit reference in this context was again (alas) to Leszek Kolakowski who labeled me a "leading ideologist of scientific technocracy." In *Conversations* I remarked that, by the same token, a professor of infectious diseases like cholera or bubonic plague ought to be called a "leading ideologist of virulent epidemics." The point is that I was not interested in what the consumptive-permissive civilization, out of its disagreeable nature, was going to do with the fruits of technology, but rather what kind of fruits this technology would bear, because—as banal as it sounds—one needs first to acquire means of mass destruction in order to execute it. In this sense nobody interested in the fate of humanity can be indifferent to the knowledge about the nature of such means, and especially not the philosopher.

As quoted in *Der Spiegel* from March 11, 1991, in England one can already purchase a phantomat for £50,000, with the advertising campaign targeting "laboratories, game arcades, architects, and the military complex." The technology has also been developed by Japanese concerns like Toshiba, Mitsubishi, Matsushita, Sharp, Sanyo, Fuji-Xerox, and Nintendo—to say nothing of the Americans and the Germans, who in 1991 held symposia on the potential of a new branch of industry capable of producing fictional reality (they continue to adhere to the name "virtual reality"). The French are not far behind, either. Thanks to an appropriate program, Prince Albert of Monaco strolled in a nonexistent English garden; others flew over seas and mountains.

On August 20, 1990, *Der Spiegel* reported that the New York publisher Simon and Schuster paid an advance of $75,000 to Howard Rheingold for a book on phantomatics, in which the most important question is to be, naturally, "Can one have sex with a computer?" Such and other attitudes were on my mind when I wrote, as quoted above, of "nightmarish social consequences" of the new information technology. One hears already about numerous people who dream about "jacking into their computer," into the world of fiction which provides unimpeded opportunities for a consumption of all possible kinds of forbidden fruits!

How did I envisage it thirty years ago? Time to introduce selected quotations (*Summa*, 1964 ed., p. 211 ff.). "Art," I wrote, is a unidirectional transfer of information. We are only addressees, only recipients of a cinematic screening or a theatrical performance. We are passive onlookers and not coparticipants in the plot. Literature does not provide the same illusion as theater does, for the reader can immediately turn to the epilogue and find out that it has already been determined. . . . In science fiction one can read sometimes about future entertainment, which is to work according to the following scenario: the hero dons the required electrodes on his head and instantaneously finds himself in the heart of the Sahara, or on the surface of Mars. Little do the authors of such depictions realize that the only difference between this 'novel' and contemporary art is an inconsequential variation on the "link-up" to the content that has been rigidly preprogrammed. Even without electrodes the illusion can be similar in a stereoscopic "circarama," possibly equipped with an additional olfactory channel beside the stereo-acoustic one. . . . Phantomatics, on the other hand, involves the creation of a *bidirectional* link-up between the artificial reality and its recipient. In other words, phantomatics is an art with feedback. It would be of course possible to hire actors, dress them up as seventeenth-century courtiers and oneself as a French monarch, and together with the troupe play out the "reign of the Louises" against an appropriate backdrop (e.g., an old castle).[5] Attempts like this are not even primitive phantomatics since, to name just one simple reason, one can always retreat from their influence.

Phantomatics means the creation of a situation where there are no "exits" from the created fiction to the real world. Let us consider one by one the means for its creation, as well as the fascinating problem of whether there is any conceivable way for the phantomatized subject to determine if his experience is only an illusion, separating him from temporarily lost reality.

Before I quote from the next chapter of *Summa* I would like to note that I have never given much attention to the philosophical aspect of the problem since, at the time of writing the book in 1961–63, I concluded that a deliberation of quasi-Berkeleyan consequences on a technology which did not yet exist was too abstract a task. I fancied I was in the situation of a man who, even before the advent of the first rickety coach with a one-cylinder engine by Mr. Ford or Mr. Benz, would have taken it upon himself to consider the terrible problems precipitated by the global expansion of transportation: the pollution of the environment, traffic jams, bottlenecks, problems with parking faced by car owners and municipal governments. There are also questions of whether such an explosion in transportation would be of any benefit at all, whether it would sooner bring profits in tourism and entertainment (e.g., from car racing), or rather dangers of a type until then unknown from history. And, if on top of that, this visionary from the mid-nineteenth century wanted to include the psychosocial effects of those jams and congestions, his oracles would surely have been received as a peculiar type of catastrophism! In much the same way I did not want to overdo my phantomology by exploiting the ontological effects of its *marketing* in the context of demand and supply. (The demand and supply are even now undergoing a phase of colossal acceleration, of billion dollar investments and technologically aroused appetites, visible in the slogan— shocking only to us—"to have sex with a computer.")

The title of the next chapter of *Summa* is "The Phantomological Machine." Here are some excerpts from it:

What can the subject experience during the link-up to the phantomatic generator? Everything. He can scale mountain cliffs or walk without a space suit or oxygen mask on the surface of the moon; in clanking armor he can lead a faithful posse to a conquest of medieval fortifications; he can explore the North Pole. He can be adulated by crowds as a winner of the Marathon, accept the Nobel Prize from the hands of the Swedish king as the greatest poet of all times, indulge in the requited love of Madame Pompadour, duel with Jason, revenge Othello, or fall under the daggers of Mafia hitmen. He can also grow enormous eagle wings and fly, or else become a fish and live his life on the coral reef; as an immense man-eater he can speed with jaws wide open after schools of prey—more! he can snatch swimming people, feast to his delight, and digest them in a tranquil nook of his underwater cavern. He can be a six-foot-four Negro or the pharaoh Amenhotep, or Attila the Hun, or contrarily, a saint or a prophet, together with an assurance that his prophecies will come true to the letter; he can die, be resurrected, and then do it again, many, many times over.

How can it be realized? It is certainly not that simple. A person's brain needs to be connected to a machine which will supply it with ocular, olfactory, tactile, and other stimuli. At the same time, the machine must instantaneously effect a split-second transfer of the stimuli generated by the brain back to its own subsystems, in response to the input impulses. There, owing to the correctional play of the feedback, as well as to the patterning of the stimuli by appropriate self-organizing systems, Miss Universe will respond to his words and kisses, the stems of flowers he grasps with his hand will flex obediently, and blood will spurt from the breast of a foe whom he fancies to stab. I beg forgiveness for the melodramatic tone of this exposition but I would like to, in as short a time and space as possible, outline the essence of phantomatics as an "art with feedback" which turns the previous recipient into an active participant and a protagonist at the center of programmed events. It is probably better to use to such vaguely operatic depictions than to indulge in technical jargon which would not only render the picture too ponderous, but would also miss the mark, since, for the time being, there are neither phantomatic machines nor their programs.

This is Lem in 1962. Because both the machine and the program now exist, I can flesh out my prediction from generally accessible publications (books on virtual reality multiply like rabbits, if not faster). To wit: in the chopper flight simulator, having donned the helmet on his head, a sensor-rigged garment on his body and sensorized gloves on his hands, the "cybernaut" beholds himself inside a helicopter cabin, in the pilot's seat. He can open the "window," he can press various buttons and move the controls in front of him that will, for example, start up the engine, or alter the angle of the rotor blades; in his "machine," his "chopper," he is going to ascend or touch down, or admire the "scenery" through the "window." The data-gloves hide inflatable elements in their lining, thanks to which the "pilot" gets an irreducible feeling of grasping the "joystick" of his "helicopter," and when he makes an adjustment, both the simulated flying vehicle and the entire external environment undergo a modification expertly imitating a real flight in all possible evolutions.

All these are no longer Lem's fantasies, for all it takes to experience them is to rent or purchase an appropriate apparatus with a suitable program. One can even get airsick from a typical sensation of being airborne, and fly not just to Seattle, but to a vomitorium as well. Is this not enough to speak of predictive accuracy? And is this not enough to conjecture that throngs of programmers must have already launched frantic efforts to achieve a simulation of the above mentioned "sex with a computer"? I readily admit that all those years ago I spared little room in *Summa* for this subject, since my main focus did not extend to haremic computerization, nor any other of its licentious forms. However, all that I have passed over will turn out to be fertile ground for phantomaticians/designers, and I fear that the erotically oriented industry will prove more profitable than one administering space walks.

Let us return to *Summa* from thirty years ago. I wrote:

The machine cannot be given a program able to anticipate all possible
actions that its recipient/protagonist might undertake. That would be
impossible. In spite of this, the machine need not have a complexity equal
to the sum of complexities of all its agents (foes, courtiers, Miss Universe,
etc.). For example, while we sleep we often find ourselves in various foreign
environments, encounter different people, sometimes peculiar, sometimes
eccentric—people who surprise us with their words, even though all of
this diverse scenery, including other participants from our reveries, is a
product of only a single dreaming brain. Thus the program of a phantomatic
fantasy may be just a general sketch of the type, "Egypt during the eleventh
dynasty," or "marine life in the Mediterranean basin." On the other hand, the
machine's memory banks must contain a complete range of data germane
to a given topic and, when the necessity arises, activate and graphically
transmit these recorded factual units. The necessity is, of course, dictated by
the very "behavior" of the phantomatized person—for example, when he
turns his head to look at that part of the pharaohs' throne chamber which
is behind his back. The impulses from his back and neck muscles which
are sent to the brain must be "countered" without delay, so that the central
projection of the optical display alters in such a way that the "back part of
the chamber" will enter his field of vision. That is because the phantomatic
machine must react instantly and adequately to every change, no matter
how minuscule, in the flow of input stimuli from the human brain.

Naturally these are, so to speak, only the first letters of the alphabet. The
laws of physiological optics, gravity, and so on must be faithfully represented
(unless they contravene the theme of the selected fantasy—e.g., somebody
wants to fly by "spreading his arms," i.e., contrary to gravity). But, apart
from the already mentioned deterministic chains of causes and effects,
the fantasy must also contain processes characterized by relative freedom.
It means simply that its internal characters—the phantomatic partners
of the protagonist—should exhibit human traits, including a (relative)
autonomy of speech and action from the acts and words of the hero; they
must not be puppets, unless even this has been demanded by the patron of
phantomization before the "show."

Of course the complexity of the employed apparatus will vary. It is easier
to imitate Miss Universe than Einstein; in the latter case the machine would
have to exhibit the complexity, and thus the intelligence, equaling the mind
of a genius. One can only hope that there will be many more aficionados of
conversing with Miss Universe than those craving to confer with the creator
of the theory of relativity.

Here I owe the reader a commentary from 1991. Despite considerable accuracy, my quoted predictions reflect a certain degree of "compression" of the qualitative differences in difficulty as far as developing programs for phantomatic shows is concerned. Miss Universe or any other silent partner of erotic nature is incomparably easier to program than any form of dialogue (as long as it is not entirely conventional, as with a telephone operator). Thirty years ago I could not see as well as I can today the colossal obstacles on the road to humanlike artificial intelligence.

The very early phase of computer development was characterized by extreme optimism as to the prospect of "computers catching up to humans." It is known at present that a program which can beat even Gary Kasparov at chess is easier to write than one which will successfully simulate a conversation with a five-year-old child. The computing power of a chess program is gigantic but, alas, so is the informational intricacy that characterizes the organism of even a small child. In contrast to the computer, the child will immediately grasp what it means to get something in its eye, sneeze because of dust, twist one's ankle, or get stung by nettle, and this almost prelinguistic knowledge is acquired en masse very early in the child's life, while the computer does not "understand" anything, so that everything must be explained to it.

Consequently, there are more difficulties on the way to interpersonal communication in phantomatics than I had been inclined to believe, even though I appreciated the differences between a fashion model and Einstein. On the other hand I overestimated problems connected to global transformations of visual contents (such as field of vision) which depend on the attitude of the phantomatee. Mistakenly I assumed that it would be necessary to collect volitional impulses from the body's nervous system, whereas the "gross" approach to people, which reflects only the essential movements of the head and limbs, is considerably simpler. Nonetheless I was right to claim in a later section of the quoted chapter that "the machine operates only on the body of facts which arrive at the brain, so that it is impossible to demand to undergo a split of personality, or an acute attack of schizophrenia."

Of essence to me was the question of "how one could determine the fictiveness of the phantomatic image." Before I return to quoting *Summa* from thirty years ago, I must record that, although the available phantomatic helmets allow stereoscopic (i.e., three-dimensional) vision, the sharpness of the image depends, as in the television screen or computer monitor, on the density of the raster grid. Since images are resolved point by point, their sharpness is not invulnerable to microscopic inspection, revealing for the time being their artificial nature. Nevertheless, the progress evident in visual technologies—evident, for example, in high definition television—gives reason to speculate that the present imperfections of the picture are only transient. In the future even a strong magnifying glass will not be able to "grain" the picture and expose its raster-made, and thus inauthentic, character. As everybody knows, the first generation Mercedes was an old cart with a sawn-off thill and, aside from its ability to move (slowly), had nothing in common with contemporary vehicles of the same make.

All the same, in my efforts to investigate differences between reality and its simulation, I contemplated the ultimate in intellectual, and not merely visual, possibilities. Thus I wrote:

Prima facie the question of difference is identical to the one asked by a person dreaming. It is true that there are dreams in which the impression of reality is entirely irresistible. It should be remembered, though, that a dreaming brain is never in as full command of its discriminatory capabilities as when awake. In ordinary circumstances a dream can appear a reality, but not the other way round (reality as a dream), unless in exceptional circumstances (e.g., immediately upon waking, or during a period of mental fatigue). But in these cases we are always dealing with a mind that can be deceived precisely because it has been "dulled."

In contrast to the dream, the phantomatic experience takes place when one is awake. It is not the brain that fabricates "other worlds" and "other people"—they are produced by the machine. As far as the quantity and content of transmitted information is concerned, a phantomatized person is a slave to the machine; he receives no other extraneous information. On the other hand he is free to do whatever he wishes with this information: he can interpret it, analyze it in all manners imaginable—that is, if he is shrewd and inquisitive enough.

One could propose that, were phantomatics to become something like the contemporary cinema, the very fact of going to the theater, buying a ticket, or performing any other preparatory activities which remain in the patron's memory during the show (such as the knowledge of who he is in real life), will entail a less than entirely serious outlook on his experience. Yet there is a double aspect to this. Conscious of the arbitrariness of the experienced actions, the person could, just as in a dream, allow himself to go much further than in reality (as a result of which his martial, social, or erotic valor would be inconsistent with his behavioral norm). This subjectively rather positive aspect of liberating one's freedom of action would, however, be controlled by the opposite one: the consciousness that neither the performed deeds, nor the characters inhabiting the fantasy, are material and true. The craving for authenticity could thus remain unsatiated after even the most superlative show.

Writing in 1991, I must digress to include facts which cannot but provoke the following reflection. Even though specialists employed by the company which programs "phantomatizers" should be the most resistant to the illusion, the fact that they are forbidden to drive for a minimum of half an hour after the simulated ride indicates that the "pressure of authenticity" created by the digital illusion must be stronger than I had once imagined. Anyway, various tricks can be accomplished on the borderline between actuality and fantasy.

Back to the past and *Summa.*

Someone goes to the phantomat and orders a trip to the Rockies. The excursion is very nice and pleasant, the show comes to its end, the assistant takes off the electrodes [in 1991 it will be a helmet—author's note] and politely bids him goodbye. The man goes out to the street and suddenly finds himself in the midst of a monstrous cataclysm; houses collapse, the earth shakes, and a big "saucer" full of Martians comes down from the sky. What happened? The awakening, the shedding the electrodes, the exit from the phantomat, were all part of the fiction which had started with the innocent nature trip.

Even if nobody played such "practical" jokes, psychiatrists would still begin to see various neurotics in their waiting rooms persecuted by phobias of a new type—the fear that what they experience is not true, that someone has imprisoned them in a "phantomatic world." I am making this remark because it clearly indicates how technology molds not only a normal mind but works its way even to the generative level of individual pathologies.

We have mentioned one of a vast number of possible ways to camouflage the "phantomaticity" of experience. One could think of a number of others, hardly less effective, not to mention the fact that each fiction can have an unlimited number of "floors"—as in sleep, when we dream that we are awake, we are just in the middle of another dream, anchored in the previous one, so to say. The "earthquake" is suddenly over, the saucer disappears, and the client realizes that he is sitting in an armchair with electrodes that connect his head to the apparatus. The politely smiling technician explains that it was all a "programming glitch"; the patron leaves, returns home, goes to sleep; the next day he goes to work only to find out that the office in which he used to work does not exist any more: it was destroyed by an explosion of an old shell from the last war.

Naturally, this *too* could be the continuation of the show. But how to find out?

To begin, there is one very simple method. As we have said before, the machine is the sole source of information about the outside world. However, it is not an exclusive source of information about the body. It performs this role only in part by replacing the body's neural mechanisms which inform it of the position of the hands, legs, head, the movement of the eyeballs, and so on. On the other hand, biochemical information supplied by the organism is not subject to control—at least in the phantomatizers discussed so far. So it is enough to do about a hundred squats, and if we begin to perspire, gasp for breath, if the heart starts to thud, and the muscles get tired, we are in reality and not in fiction, because the muscle fatigue has been precipitated by an accumulation of lactic acid. The machine cannot influence the level of sugar in blood, nor the levels of carbon dioxide in it, nor the concentration of the lactic acid in muscles. In a phantomatic illusion one could do even a thousand squats without any signs of exhaustion. But there is a way to circumvent even that—the phantomatized person might be granted freedom of movement.

Addendum from 1991: this is already being done, and the observers of people undergoing such visions find their behavior quite droll and bizarre. The reason is the same which I mentioned in *Summa:* "If the phantomatized person reached for a sword, only the motion would be true, because from the point of view of an outside observer his hand would be grasping the void."

This is exactly what is happening, only now the hand must be embedded in a glove armed with sensors and inflatable cushions.

Back to the book:

The ultimate test is the "intellectual contest with the machine." The probability of being able to distinguish a session from reality depends on the "phantomatic potential" of the machine. Let us say that you are looking for an indication of whether you are in the authentic reality. You may know some famous psychologist or philosopher, so you pay him a visit and engage him in conversation. It could be an illusion, but the machine that imitates a sentient interlocutor must be significantly more complex than one which dishes out scenes from soap operas, like the one with the landing of a Martian saucer. In fact, the phantomat for "travel" and the phantomat that "creates people" are two different contraptions. Constructing the latter is immeasurably more difficult than the former.

Truth can be also investigated differently. Like every human being, you have your own secrets. They might be banal, but they are intimately your own. The machine cannot "read thoughts" (that is impossible: the memory's neural code is a person's individual property, and even if "cracked" it would reveal nothing of other people's codes). So neither the machine, nor anybody else, knows that a certain drawer in your desk is warped. Your hurry back to the house and check whether that is the case. The stuck drawer makes the reality of your world extremely probable. The creator of the program would have had to be a master of espionage to discover and put on magnetic tapes even such a trifle as a warped drawer! It would appear that an illusion could be most readily exposed by analogous details. Still, the machine always has the opportunity of a tactical maneuver. The drawer is not stuck. You realize that you are still inside a fantasy. Your wife appears whom you pronounce to be only an "illusion." Laughing with sympathy, she reveals to you that a carpenter she called that morning fixed the drawer. Once again nothing is certain. Either this world is real, or the machine has performed a cunning maneuver, countering your move.

Another addendum from 1991. The reason for quoting so extensively from a book of prognoses from thirty years ago is that these prognoses gain credence from present-day trends. As proven by the worldwide munificence of investment stretching from the United States to Japan, great numbers of large corporations and great numbers of experts are gearing up for the large-scale production of "phantomats," as well as for research into market niches where these can be employed. One can therefore expect in this last decade of our millennium a veritable deluge of products for generating synthetic reality. It will turn out to be no small competition to drug consumption, so extraordinarily harmful to the social and medical health of the society. Moreover it is going to be the first surrogate technology able to rival reality in experience and sensation, able to fulfill all dreams, including (alas) even the most obscene or sadistic ones. I find it difficult to believe in a great but unfulfilled demand for Nobel Prize–granting ceremonies, especially if there are no special reasons for meriting the award.

I restrict myself only to my own ideas simply because, with the exception of several articles from scientific and popular press, I am not familiar with any sources from the already rather substantial library on that subject (I am not referring to the chimeras of science fiction, but to serious and factual information and/or extrapolation). It is not impossible that more inquisitive and socially mature ideas are being born even this very moment; however, as my sources in the United States report, purely technical aspects win over any philosophical or future-oriented analyses of the consequences of this technology. One could claim, however, that we are dealing with a technology of solipsistic creation: the totality of experience derived from such informationally concentrated and canned worlds *is* the exclusive property of individuals who hook themselves up to such generators. It is true that a "phantomatic abduction" is today nothing more than a possibility, but even as such it merits examination. Here is what I wrote in 1962:

> One must not go to the other extreme. In a phantomatic world every not-so-ordinary event will lead to a suspicion that it is a manufactured fiction, because one can become "phantomatized" while asleep. And yet even in the real world, old shells sometimes blow up, and wives summon carpenters. We must therefore accept that a statement of the type "A person *X* is in the real and not in a phantomatic world," can only be made with a certain probability, which can be exceedingly high, but can never achieve absolute certainty. A contest with the machine is like a game of chess: a contemporary computer will lose to a grand master but will beat a mediocre player. The same thing can be said of phantomats. The fundamental weakness of all efforts to discover the true state of affairs lies in the fact that the person who questions the authenticity of the world he lives in is forced to act alone. This is because turning to other people for help would be, or at least could be, an act of *giving the machine strategically valuable information*. If this is only an illusion, confiding in an old friend about problems of existential uncertainty might impart to the machine additional information which it will use to strengthen one's conviction about the reality of the experience.

Insert from 1991: the assumption of such a strategy on the part of the machine did not spring from my paranoid persecution mania, but simply from the same reasons which drive programmers to refine computer chess strategies until they triumph with increasing consistency over human grand masters. It is, generally speaking, a drive to equal nature itself in creative resourcefulness—a drive so human that it requires no special rationalizations. Back to Lem, 1962:

> Therefore the "player" cannot trust anybody but himself, which seriously constrains his range of options. He is more or less forced to remain on the defensive for he *could be* completely surrounded. What obtains is that the phantomatic world is a world of total solitude. There can be no more than a single person in it—in the same way that it is not possible for two real people to find themselves in the same dream.
>
> Thus no civilization can phantomatize itself completely. If, from a certain moment on, all of its members began to live inside phantomatic visions, the real world of that civilization would come to a halt and die out. Since even the most delicious phantomatic dishes would not sustain life functions (although appropriate impulses could create an impression of gratification), a phantomatized person would still have to receive authentic meals.
>
> Naturally one can imagine some kind of panplanetary "Superphantomat" to which the inhabitants of the planet would be connected "once and for all," that is, till the end of their lives, while the physiological processes of their bodies were sustained by automatic devices (e.g., by introducing proper nutritional formulae directly into the blood). This "paradised" civilization obviously appears to be a nightmare. Such criteria cannot, however, determine its likelihood. It would be decided by something else. The civilization would exist only for the lifespan of a single generation, the one connected to the Superphantomat. It would be thus a singular instance of euthanasia, a form of prolonged, collective suicide. For this reason its implementation may be regarded as impossible.

The reflections on the Superphantomat were to demonstrate the extremity from which the manufacture of synthetic realities will most probably shy away. Nevertheless, what is at stake is an incipient type of industry that can delude people, leading them terribly astray with promises of counterfeit bounty. In another chapter of *Summa* I wrote:

> According to my system of classification, phantomatics can be peripheral or central. The former acts on the brain indirectly, in the sense that the phantomatizing stimuli only provide information about facts, in an analogy to reality. A peripheral phantomat determines external, but not internal states, because *the same* sensory perceptions (e.g., a thunderstorm, or sitting atop a pyramid), no matter if generated artificially or naturally, will

precipitate different feelings, emotions, or reactions in different people. On the other hand, central phantomatics works through a specific and direct agitation of the brain, and not through the intermediary of neural sensory paths . . .

Phantomatics appears to be a sort of pinnacle toward which sundry forms and technologies of entertainment converge. There are already houses of illusion, ghost houses, funhouses—Disneyland is in fact one big primitive pseudophantomat. Apart from these variations, permitted by law, there are illicit ones (this is the situation in Jean Genet's *Balcony* where the site of pseudophantomatization is a brothel). Phantomatics has a certain potential to become an art. At least that would be my initial concession. This could therefore lead it to a split into artistically valuable product and mediocre kitsch, as with the movies or various other types of art.

The menace of phantomatics is, however, incomparably greater than that represented by debased cinema, which sometimes crosses the boundaries of social norms, for example, in its pornographic or sadistic incarnations. For, due to its specificity, phantomatics offers the kind of experience which, in its intimacy, is equaled only by a dream.

Added in 1991: The knowledge of the program of the phantomatic illusion does not necessarily suffice to deduce the actions of a particular user of the phantomat within the framework of the program, all because the program *must* be quite general in its nature. It is much the same when the plan of a maze does not suffice to deduce the particular route of the person who has taken it. This can be observed even today, albeit on a small, innocuous scale. Thus whoever fails to open the pseudowindow in the helicopter simulator will not see the panoramic view during the flight; whoever fails to run into an obstacle in a driving simulator will not experience a mock crash. One could legislate the privacy of such fantasies which would guarantee that the reactions of the phantomatized subject would not be systematically surveyed and recorded. That rule would apply to all cases where phantomatization is *not* a part of some test, for example, to examine the skills of a pilot, surgeon, or car driver.

In this sense [1962] we are dealing with a technology of surrogate wish-fulfillment, quite prone to be abused through actions which contravene a socially permissible norm. Some people might maintain that such phantomatic licentiousness could not be socially dangerous; on the contrary, it could be something akin to a "release." After all, doing evil unto others during a session does not harm anyone. Is anybody held accountable for the most horrible contents of their dreams? Is it not better that someone might assault or even murder his adversary in a phantomat, instead of doing it in reality? Or "lust after his brother's wife," which otherwise could easily bring calamity on some quiet couple?

In other words, is it possible for phantomatics to accommodate, without harming anyone, the dark forces lurking in man? This attitude can be contrasted with an opposite one. A critic might argue that criminal acts committed during the fantasy would only encourage the patron to repeat them in real life. As we all know, people place most value on what they cannot get. Such contrariness is evident at every step. In reality it is not rationally defensible. What really motivates a collector to give away everything for an authentic Van Gogh that, without the help of an army of experts, he will not be able to tell from an impeccable forgery anyway? A quest for "authenticity." In the same manner the inauthenticity of the phantomatic experience would rob it of the "buffer" quality; it would instead become a school and a training ground for perfecting socially forbidden acts, rather than their "absorber." Once the phantomatic illusion is indistinguishable from reality, it could lead to incalculable consequences. After committing a murder, a killer could defend himself by declaring that, to the best of his knowledge, the whole thing had been a "phantomatic illusion." Apart from that, many people might become so entangled in the indistinguishability of truth and fiction, in a subjectively inseparable world of authenticity and illusion, that they could never find a way out of this maze. Such situations would truly become powerful generators of frustrations and psychic breakdowns.

It thus appears that there are portentous reasons against recognizing phantomatics as a domain of complete freedom of action à la dream, in which frenzies of nihilistic obscenities would be limited only by imagination. Of course there might also appear illegal phantomatic productions. This, however, is more a problem for the police than for cybernetics. From programmers one could demand construction of a sort of V-chip (analogous to the Freudian "dream censor") that would arrest the fantasy as soon as the subject betrayed any aggressive, sadistic, or other negative tendencies.

It would appear that this is a purely technical problem (controlling the relay of stimulating—relative to regulating—information). If someone is able to construct the phantomat, the introduction of such controls should not be too hard, right? At this point we must, however, consider a couple of completely unexpected consequences of such putative controls. Let us start with the simpler one. It is clear that phantomatization of a vast majority of works of art would not be possible: they would have to be placed outside the permitted limits. . . . If the protagonist of a session expresses even so guileless a wish as to become Podbipięta, there is no way to avoid evil for, as Podbipięta, he will slay three Turks in one stroke, or as Hamlet he will stab Polonius as a rat.[6] And if—I beg pardon for this example—he desires to experience the martyrdom of some saint, that too could carry some peculiar overtones. The point is not only that works in which nobody kills or harms anybody else are few and far between (this includes children's stories—how bloody are the Grimm brothers' tales!). What matters is that the range of stimuli control, the "censorship" of the phantomat, does not extend at all to the proper sphere of the phantomatized person's experience. Maybe he craves flogging out of a need for religious martyrdom, or maybe he is just an ordinary masochist. At most one can control what stimuli enter the brain, but not what happens in the brain, and what it feels. The content of the experience simply remains outside control. (In this particular case it would seem to be a minus, even though in principle we may agree that it is very fortuitous.) Even the rather modest experimental material, obtained by stimulating certain parts of the human brain (during surgery), indicates that in every brain the same, or similar, input is encoded differently.

The language used by neurons to communicate with our brains is virtually the same in all people, while the language, or the form of encoding, of memories and connotative loops, is highly individualistic. This is easy to demonstrate, since memories organize themselves in a particular way only for single individuals. Thus some associate pain with elevated suffering and retribution for transgressions, while for others it is a source of perverse enjoyment. In this way we have attained the limits of phantomatics, because one cannot with its aid directly determine opinions, beliefs, or feelings. It is possible to mold the pseudomaterial content of experience, but not the accompanying judgments, assessments, thoughts, sentiments, and associations. For this reason I called this technology "peripheral." It is similar to real life where, from two identical situations, two individuals can derive quite different, if not contrary conclusions, both in the emotional and experiential sense. Even though *nihil est in intellectu quod non prius fuerit in sensu* (in phantomatics rather *in nervo*), neural stimulation does not uniquely determine the resulting intellectual-emotional states.[7] (A cyberneticist would say: the "input" and "output" states do not uniquely determine the state of the system between them.)

How is it possible, somebody could object? Didn't we say before that phantomatics enables one to "experience everything," even, say, being a crocodile or a fish?

A crocodile or a shark, for sure, but only in "play-acting," and for two reasons. First, it is play-acting because it is only an illusory fiction, as we already know. Second, because to be really a crocodile one must have a crocodile, and not a human, brain. Ultimately a person can only be himself. This must nevertheless be understood correctly. If a clerk at the National Bank dreams of becoming a clerk at the Bank of Investments, his wish can be fulfilled perfectly. If, on the other hand, he desires to become Napoleon Bonaparte for a couple of hours, he will be so (during the show) only externally. If he looks in the mirror he will see Bonaparte's face, he will be surrounded by a "trusty corps" of loyal marshals, but he will not be able to converse with them in French if he did not speak that language before. Also, as Bonaparte, he will not exhibit Napoleon's traits of character as known from history, but his own. At most he will "play" Napoleon, imitating him with better or worse results. The same applies to the crocodile.

Phantomatics can let a graphomaniac receive the Nobel Prize for his oratory; during the show the entire world may throw itself at his feet, everybody will adulate him for his masterpieces, but he still will not be able to write them, unless somebody puts them on his desk.

We could put it this way: the more remote the historical time and the personality type of the assumed character from the patron's own time and disposition, the more common, naive, and primitive the form of behavior he will display (as long as it depends, of course, on his activity). To be crowned a king, or to entertain a papal nuncio, one needs to be familiar with the proper ceremonial, and the most that can happen is that the agents created by the illusion can pretend not to see the idiotic stunts of the ermine-clad clerk of the National Bank. Maybe these lapses will not diminish his satisfaction, but elements of triviality and clowning in the entire situation should be plain to see. For this reason it is difficult to expect phantomatics to become a mature form of art in the full sense of the word. Beside the large but separate domain of its useful applications which have nothing to do either with entertainment or art, it will probably become above all an entertainment, a kind of "Super Globetrotter," able to roam through the possible and impossible cosmos.

One can, nonetheless, use phantomatics to create educational or training situations of the highest quality. One can instruct phantomatically in all kinds of professions—from the medical, engineering, or aeronautical, down to the job of a detective, spy, or alpinist. As such there is no danger of accident, plane crash, tragedy at the operating table, or a catastrophe caused by an ill-calculated construction. Moreover, in this way we can also study psychological reactions, which can be especially valuable in professions with a high degree of risk and stress, for example, astronautics. A method of disguising the onset of illusion will allow the creation of conditions in which the subject will not know whether he is flying to the moon for real or in fiction. The disguise will be recommended (and justified) in cases where there is a need for an *automatic* reaction in the face of a real emergency, and not a fictive one where demonstrating one's personal courage comes so easily to everyone.

"Phantomatic tests" will enable psychologists better to understand human attitudes and reactions over a very broad spectrum, as well as to analyze the mechanisms of the origins of panic, depression, and other emotional states. They will enable an accelerated selection of candidates for various programs, degrees, and professions. Furthermore phantomatics can make bearable years of solitude—on a planetary or even stellar voyage. To those on the flight, this technology will allow an almost "normal" life, for example, touring Earth (who knows, maybe even sea baths, etc.), owing to some appropriately sophisticated mechanism. They will also listen to lectures conducted by outstanding teachers. [Thanks to expert programs, the level of education could indeed rise to the highest peaks—Lem, addendum from 1991].

For paraplegics, bedridden patients, convalescents, phantomatics can be as much of a blessing as for old people wishing to experience a second youth. In this sense the entertainment function could, although not necessarily, prove marginal in comparison to more socially significant ones.

No doubt this new branch of the information industry will also have a negative reaction. There will emerge groups of fervent opponents, devotees of authenticity who will disdain such spuriousness of experience. Still, I think [in 1962] that sensible compromises will pave the way because, ultimately, the goal of every dynamic civilization is to make life easier, and its development is marked to a large extent by the broadening of the range of things which *do* make life easier. Naturally phantomatics could also become a menace, a social plague, but this possibility applies to all technological artifacts (albeit not to the same degree). The extent of detriment versus utility is a problem that cuts into the essence of social formations, political persuasions, and faith.

Phantomatics will be their dependent variable, though not necessarily a function (in the mathematical sense).

I am writing this last sentence in 1991 to conclude with the following remark. The price catalogs of companies producing systems of virtual-reality devices list such items as Eye-Phone (price: $9,400), Data-Glove

($8,800), VPL package (complete for $220,000). At the same time the advertisers assure that the heavy Eye-Phone has eighty-six thousand pixels, while the Data-Glove is synchronically connected alongside each finger to the apparatus that makes the whole work in real time, so that the phantomatee does not observe the slightest delay between his movements and the appropriate changes in vision or other senses. I must not and I do not want to turn the end of this article into an advertisement. But the above quoted data from 1990 confirm that the beginnings of what I called phantomatics are no longer just a utopian mistake nor a fictive fairy tale, but accurate prediction. What then does a philosopher do when preparing a contemporary selection of his essays from thirty years ago? In keeping with the title of his reprinted anthology, *In Praise of Inconsistency,* Kolakowski calmly reiterates that everything that Lem had concocted in 1963–64 is a fib.[8]

Stanislaw Lem—Kraków, May 1991

Translated by Peter Swirski

Notes

1. Published in Poland by Wydawnictwo Literackie in 1964; expanded in a 1967 edition.

2. Leszek Kolakowski is one of the more eminent Polish philosophers of the postwar period.

3. London: Unwin, 1946.

4. "An Extra Dimension of Realism for Games Arcades," *New Scientist* 130 (1991): 23.

5. This setup is the subject of one of Lem's stories from *A Perfect Vacuum,* entitled "Gruppenführer Louis XVI."

6. Podbipięta is a knight, an important character in *Ogniem i mieczem,* one of the classic Polish novels by a 1905 Nobel Prize–winning writer, Henryk Sienkiewicz (1846–1916).

7. The Latin phrase can be translated, "Nothing enters the mind before it has passed through the senses."

8. London: Puls, vol. 3 (42–51).

Lem in a Nutshell
[Written Interview with Stanislaw Lem, July 1994]

Stanislaw Lem: The questions which you have submitted touch on so many issues that the answer to each and every one of them would require from me a separate monograph, if not an entire book. Moreover it is possible that my answers may not add up to a cogent whole, since I do not have at my command a perfectly homogenized and distilled "system of thought." In many of the problems discussed here my opinions may therefore fail to intersect, or perhaps may even seem mutually contradictory. Put simply, *I do not see myself as subjectively infallible.* That is to say, I am not dogmatic about a fundamental correctness of my views, not only because my views have evolved over the years, but also because I must acknowledge my ignorance of many areas of knowledge, some of which I am only poorly (inadequately) acquainted with. This admission, here in the introduction, is not a result of any "hedging," or of false modesty, but a sober report on the state of my mental capacities.

Peter Swirski: *What are your views on scientific realism/empiricism? Is there a reference to outside reality (nature), or are we in the grip of scientific constructivism? To what degree are our theories anthropomorphic and contingent constructions? Or are we perhaps approaching these epistemological questions in terms of outdated dichotomies? Is there progress and continuity in science and its theories? What role does (or should) "pure" research play in scientific pursuits?*

Lem: Irrespective of the quality and significance of any critique of scientific empiricism and rationalistic realism, there is *nothing* better to unseat them from their place. All types of revelations, specific to various religious systems, are in reality nothing but cross-generational messages from a distant past, and their very diversity and multiplicity manifests to me their essential cognitive arbitrariness. Faced with this whole array of dogmatic systems, one must put one's trust in empirical science. There is only one and unique science; moreover, it is the only system which is ready to acknowledge its own errors and shortcomings, even while trying to rectify them by means of better, more comprehensive knowledge.

One is often asked to choose between the following polarities: 1) science points "directly" (in the referential sense) to nature, or 2) science is nothing but constructivism which takes advantage of mathematics, as the most exact form of language, to construct models of the world (e.g., in physics).

To me, the most satisfying stance between these two extremes is one of moderation. Nature can never be known directly: the neopositivist's plain facts (data) are accessible to the human sensorium, but they are not accessible in a way that would be transhumanly, or suprahumanly, "objective." Science perceives facts through theories, and theories through facts, and this relationship may sometimes seem like a *circulus vitiosus*. However, even though it is not omnipotent, science does everything in its power to break out of this circle. The explosive surge in knowledge during the last centuries confirms that this effort is occasionally crowned with success, even if only a partial one.

There is no doubt that, to a certain extent at least, all of our theories must be anthropomorphic. Our brain owes its intersubjective cognitive powers to *language*. All present linguistic theories are, in my view, guilty of radical simplifications of the state of linguistic conditions which arose in the course of evolution. Up to and including David Hilbert, mathematics had been carrying out a continuous campaign against polysemy, marshaling its logical skills to root out the "fuzzy" polyvalence of natural language. However, Gödel's discovery of the incompleteness of mathematical systems put an end to Hilbert's belief in, and hopes for, the axiomatization of mathematics. In a very intriguing sense, there appears to be some correspondence between the facts of physics and the facts established by Gödel's discovery. In the same way that the part of the universe penetrated and explored macroscopically by Einstein's theories (especially the General Theory) *breaks down* in black holes, the logically absolute provability of all statements in all mathematical systems *breaks down* as soon as it encounters "mathematical holes" in the shape of true propositions which originate within the system, yet whose truth can be proven only by means of a system which is "richer," that is, hierarchically superior. (I must note with regret that the answer to just your first question has already become a small lecture, but in truth it was a whole collection of questions.)

Classical logic fails especially (though not only) in quantum mechanics, since "complementarity" (as it was developed by Niels Bohr) is an attempt to avoid stating explicitly that in certain "places" our theories do not suffice, forcing us to fall back on metaphors (such as, for example, "complementarity"). This shows once again that man as *Homo sapiens*—counting more or less from the Neanderthals—is equipped with a brain adapted specifically to survival in the earthly environment, that is, somewhere between macroscopic and microscopic scales (cosmos and quanta). As a consequence our means of cognition are insufficient to penetrate fully all those aspects of the world which did not contribute to the progress of our "encephalization."

Science is inherently programmed to eradicate anachronistic dichotomies. Take, for example, the old confrontation between preformism and epigenetics in biology: today we already know that *tertium datur*.[1] All the same, it is getting increasingly difficult to eliminate such dichotomies because our minds resist it, craving simplicity and thus *reductionism* of everything that can be reduced. Progress (conceived here in terms of expansion of knowledge) in the hard sciences is undeniable, but without the implication of continuity. New theories are not merely more precise, more detailed versions of theories from the past; they involve fundamental paradigmatic changes (cf. the physics of Newton and Einstein, or the latter before and after Heisenberg's quantum mechanics).

And last: it is absolutely crucial to remember that without basic, even if currently "useless," research, sooner or later science will atrophy through stagnation. People who fail to realize this should never be put in charge of governmental treasuries, for fear of inflicting damage on their countries on the global scale.

Swirski: *Are you a materialist? Do you agree that the "stuff" of the universe is ultimately information? What do you make of the stunning parallels between the theorems of Einsteinian (gravitational) physics and those of logic-driven information theory? What do you think of the comparisons between "selfish" genes which you (and, later, Dawkins) described, and "memes"—ideas which are also amenable to description in game theoretic terms of survival in a hostile and competitive environment?*

Lem: The concept of materialism is polyvalent to a high degree. If one contrasts it with solipsism, this entire binary polarity becomes nonsensical. The world exists without us, and solipsism is simply ludicrous, even though it is true that a "world" dies with each one of us. Most probably, when subjected to compression, matter can exist continuously only within certain limited values of parameters such as time, gravity, and space. Maybe matter is annihilated in black holes, and maybe it only undergoes a form of intercosmic "transfer." Although truly we don't know what we don't know, it does not mean that *ignoramus et ignorabimus*.[2]

No, I do not think information is the ultimate building block ("stuff") of the universe. I have already mentioned the parallels between Einsteinian physics and Gödelian collapse in language (nota bene I regard Gödel's proof as a constant for the entire metagalaxy, perhaps even the entire universe). Anyway, this parallelism becomes less startling if only we recognize that we, the "children" of the cosmos, bear the proof of this genealogy in ourselves, besides perceiving it in the world outside ourselves.

Now, as for genes: they are not 100 percent selfish; that was, both for Dawkins and myself, a certain one-sided exaggeration of their evolutionary status. At the same time, "junk DNA" has been recently recognized to be at least partly a new type of stabilizer and "assistant" of structural genes (and morphogenes) within a chromosome. However, all this is a result of studies which are still very much in progress. Memes, on the other hand, don't exist literally in the same way that genes do. They cannot, for example, be isolated. The issue here is a certain contamination of concepts with metaphors, for what Dawkins called a meme, and what someone else might perhaps call an archetype, is only a kind of configuration of stereotypically activated neural structures in the brain (even if allowing for possibly significant deviations in individual cases). One cannot isolate memes, just as one cannot isolate engrams; these "elements" of brain configuration are not discoverable, because they do not exist as isolated entities.[3] They can be projected as various computer models, but only in the semantic and not in the topological sense.

Does survival in a hostile environment result through natural selection in the creation of memes? I don't know. The fact that certain molecules, for example, hemes of hemoglobin, are almost identical not only in all mammals but in all vertebrates, cannot be used here as an argument for the universality of memes. Survival strategies can be similar or not; even though, as Feyerabend says, anything goes at this point, as long as it serves the cause of survival, it does not automatically entail the conclusion that this "anything" must be identical.

Swirski: *Are we about to be overwhelmed by the information crisis? Does computerization of inquiry necessarily entail loss of control over studied phenomena? Has human civilization taken any irretrievable steps in its cultural/technological evolution? Is intuition the only tool in directing future scientific research, or do we have any more formal means of predicting where to concentrate thinning resources?*

Lem: I think it is quite possible that we will be overwhelmed by the "information crisis." The sense in which it may become possible is determined by the connotations with which we designate "crisis." "Information highway" is a very shaky undertaking for this reason: people all over the world, *in and out of themselves,* have nothing to communicate to one another that might turn the "epistolographic era" into an outmoded concept, destined for oblivion. Even the Internet has already been invaded by various maniacal or malevolent hackers, not to say anything about pornographers. The discomfort, as one of the effects of paninformational omnipresence, can be worse than the compensating comfort, that is, the ability to inform a fisherman in Normandy of the latest round of baseball scores from Arizona. Informational inundation has already come to pass; now the proliferation of satellites generates greater and greater redundancy.

Whoever owns ten suits, has only ten suits to choose from; whoever owns ten department stores full of clothing must, in practice, choose for himself a few garments to wear, and will hardly gain from it at all. It is possible to get drunk with information. It can become a narcotic. I think information ought to be directed into relatively closed circuits, a trend which is already realized in banks, stock market exchanges, scientific establishments, universities, and libraries. Two hundred satellite programs on television is a surfeit impossible to take advantage of. This already qualifies as an information deluge.

I hypothesized once in one of my fictions (I think it was in *On Site Inspection*) that the environment could become more intelligent than its inhabitants. Theoretically speaking, if we indulge in a linear extrapolation of computer processing power, it certainly begins to look like it could happen. Will this derail (stunt) the gnostic and epistemic potential of humanity? It is too hard to predict. Perhaps it will, and perhaps it won't; all depends on the trajectory of the future evolution not of human beings but of computers. Man appears to be the terminal product of a certain evolutionary path which, from hominid through hominid, had given rise to the only species still surviving today, *Homo sapiens*. Autoevolution of *Homo sapiens* seems to me possible; I have written grotesques on this subject as early as *The Star Diaries*, even if only to illustrate possible hazards, and not as a serious prediction of superhuman development. What I am trying to say is that, in the process of a progressive amplification of man's wisdom, one can envision various corrective steps, but not an all-out race against computer evolution. In any case, that would be a blind alley, I think. We have no use for supergenius "production lines."

I don't know if we have already entered the technological foxhole. Maybe so, maybe not. One thing is clear though: without a halt to the demographic explosion, the twenty-first and twenty-second centuries will gradually have to marshal all our *global* scientific and technological resources against this demographic deluge, or (if we follow the advice of the Vatican) it will eventually drown human civilization. We are talking here about different types of evil and of the difficult choices among them. It is true that you can't have a cake and eat it too; on the other hand, I could not tell you if the point of no return has been crossed yet, although there are many signs pointing in this direction.

What of our management of the future? We must disavow neither intuition, nor any of the more rational, more deliberately formulated goals and strategies. Here, too, the middle ground—or better still, complementarity—looks like the optimal strategy in the long run. Incidentally, this is also the reason that democracy (as a system) will find itself more and more at a disadvantage. Why? Simply because it is impossible to hold any referenda in the field of human knowledge; for example, to decide in a national plebiscite whether to support or repress scientific research into eugenics, into the human genome project, whether to treat cancer surgically or chemically, and so on. The society must delegate the domain of choice to a highly select group of experts, even though we all know that even experts from one discipline rarely agree with one another (for a relevant example one might look to the use of atomic energy, but this is already a subject for a separate book). We can find innovative ways to replace our perishable resources, but only to a certain extent. Here I am a moderate optimist. The era of conventional fossil fuels or even thermonuclear power can be, however, only a transitional stage on the road to technobiocenosis (I described it in some of my prognoses; unfortunately, they were published only in Germany).[4] Our resources will serve us for centuries to come, *if* we manage to put a stop to the demographic explosion.

Swirski: *Is chance just our ignorance of underlying causes (tychism)? What about certain empirical results which seem to indicate that chance (random) events may be somehow related temporally? Why are most—if not all—human cultural formations (religion, theosophy, metaphysics, social theory) based ultimately on deterministic models of the universe? What do you think of Roger Penrose's theory from* The Emperor's New Mind[5] *according to which quantum theory is only an approximation to the classical-cum-quantum picture of the universe?*

Lem: Accident, or chance, is a general term which comprises a very diverse range of phenomena. Science, like any other domain of human activity, is subject to the coming and passing of fads and fashions. These days what's "in" are fractals (Benoit Mandelbrot) and chaos, that is, a kind of contaminated determinism. The categories here are very fluid. Causality seems to reach its limits in mega- and nanodimensions; we do not understand the causes of the Big Bang, nor of such acausal phenomena as radioactive decay (e.g., alpha and beta in atomic nuclei), which are determined only statistically. It is wrong to resolve what we do not yet precisely understand under the causal/acausal guillotine, and thus pronounce accident (chance) as a solution to the problem.

Mathematics recognizes many forms of chance: there are Markov's chains of various complexity (but without "memory"—those with memory are no longer Markov's chains), and there are many types of stochastic probability.[6] Before the twentieth century probability had been considered an *illegitime natum* child of mathematics; today it turns out to be an ever more dominating facet in all directions of research in pure mathematics. As far as causality is concerned, any dichotomy should be applied here with a great deal of caution; even if it may be useful today, tomorrow it could be replaced by a more fundamental kind of formalism. This problem has been studied in more detail by the esteemed Russian expert on probability, Vasilii Nalimov (at least one of his books is available in the English translation; I know because I have a copy myself).[7]

The most recent experimental and theoretical results seem to indicate that physical reality is both local and nonlocal. Its nonlocal character is supported, among others, by the experimental confirmation of the so-called Einstein-Podolsky-Rosen (EPR) paradox. On the other hand, locality is underwritten by the entire body of physics which, as a consequence of the limiting (and thus finite) speed of light, negates the possibility of *simultaneous* events that may be connected informationally or energetically over arbitrarily long distances. The human mind registers here an obvious logical contradiction which, all the same, prevents in a very subtle way a transfer of information by means of the EPR method. In a somewhat anthropomorphic way, it looks as if nature aimed to deflect the head-on collision of the two sides of the coin, with the heads as local, and the tails as nonlocal causality. It seems that this could somehow relate to the chance/determinism dichotomy. As to whether the limiting categories of accidental versus deterministic chance really exist (incidentally, the latter would be just a result of our ignorance), the debate rages on. Anyway, I must stop here since this topic also could easily become another book.

In the latest edition of my *Philosophy of Chance*, the first chapter bears the title "Limits to Cultural Growth" ("Granice wzrostu kultury"). I have remarked in it that both religion and science started out with models of *deterministic* nature; yet in the course of its development, under the pressure of experimental data, science underwent a conversion which led to its gradual renunciation of strict determinism. In contrast, religious faith, indifferent to empirical experiment and factual duplication, has been conducive to the reinforcement of determinism. For example, just as in Buddhism one could not fail to undergo metempsychosis as a result of chance, it never could happen in Christianity that, due to a chance "error," Providence might send to paradise someone whom it had intended to go to hell. The reckoning of religious faith is deterministic right in its essence. I do not know if anybody ever tried to investigate, for example, Greek mythology (e.g., the Olympic sagas) from the perspective of accident and chance, but the idea would seem worth the effort.

Now, Penrose: acquiescence to his hypothesis depends on how one understands (interprets) the meaning of the term "approximate." If we are to consider Newton's theory of gravity as an approximation to Einstein's, then the answer will be affirmative. However, I do not think that approximation should be applied so broadly. On the contrary, I am inclined to think that if a Grand Unified Theory (what I half-seriously called the General Theory of Everything) ever sees the light of day—which is far from certain—it will be nothing like a hybrid of our classical and quantum theories but something else still, something completely different. These, however, are only my conjectures, by the nature of things not open to proof.

The occasional voices today, proclaiming that physics might allegedly be approaching the end of its progress, are nothing new. Toward the end of the nineteenth century, the then contemporary physicists entertained a similar type of anxiety, fearing that there would be nothing left for the physicists of the twentieth century to work on. Such reactions are very shortsighted, albeit understandable. The scientist *cannot* (partly for psychological reasons) regard his own theoretical contributions as purely transient. On the other hand, thanks to the passing of old theories, which are ill-suited to the surrounding world (somewhat in the manner of the "bio-evolutionary method"), their place can be occupied by better and more adequate theories.

Swirski: *How would you describe yourself as a philosopher, in terms of the philosophy of science? Is there a philosopher with whom you feel special affinity? Would it be Russell? Do you regard the work of contemporary academic philosophy—for example analytical aesthetics—as sterile? Why isn't there any "progress" in ethical theory which lags further and further behind social reality? Does philosophy of science have any practical bearing on the practice and progress of science, or is it an independent discipline?*

Lem: Together with Bernd Gräfrath, a philosopher from the Essen University, we have come up with "philosophy of the future" as a designation for my brand of philosophy. Its essence can be expressed as an analytic effort to investigate how, under pressure from future empirical knowledge, philosophy (ontology, epistemology, aesthetics, ethics) will *have to* change in response. In a way this is similar to what happened to the Aristotelian philosophy when it had to retreat from the study of—to take one example—the planets and the firmament, leaving these areas of inquiry to the hard (in the Popperian sense) sciences. At the same time, there are philosophies like phenomenology or existentialism which, under such pressure, would clearly undergo a shift in the direction of religious faiths, especially godless ones, like Buddhism.

In general, one clear pattern emerges from a historical investigation of philosophy of science: the more recent a period one considers, the more evident it becomes how philosophers were forced to modify their views under pressure from factual data provided by the sciences. In contrast, other branches of philosophy—here phenomenology can serve as a good example—I include Hegel, Heidegger, Derrida, Lyotard, et alia—progressively distanced themselves from scientific knowledge, forsaking altogether the appeal to experimental tests and hypotheses on which science rests. This trend had a curious corollary in the fact that both Husserl and Heidegger wrote *only* first volumes of their major systemic works. Following an evolution in their thinking, they clearly could no longer write successive volumes in the spirit of the first. There were also others, like Wittgenstein, who in the first half of his life produced *Tractatus Logico-Philosophicus*, only to demolish it in his later writings. . . . Anyway, Bertrand Russell is one of the few philosophers whom I consistently rate very highly.

I do not indulge in any intensive reading of philosophy. I unquestionably regard it as a derivative of science; to me nonexperimental speculations of the human mind are not its highest instance of cognition. Hypotheses *must* be brought to a confrontation with experiment, that is, they must be falsifiable, despite all the dilemmas interwoven with the uncertainties of the falsification procedures (which Feyerabend or Imre Lakatos brought into focus by underscoring the imperfections of the Popperian method and its criterion of falsifiability). At the same time, when these hypothesis-buttressed experiments "settle" into mathematical structures of our theories and models, the logico-mathematical form of these very structures can give rise to a very wide range of interpretations (semantic designates) by different schools of physicists. At this point philosophers can only select the school which they will follow. It is important to remember that those among them who insist on maintaining their "independence" from science often fail to realize (like Derrida) that *no* school of philosophy can completely avoid Gödel and the consequences of his famous proofs (there were, in fact, two proofs, although the second one is partially implicated in the first).

Philosophy of science must perforce be subservient to the labors and fruits of science. It is a sociological fact that philosophy of science is pursued—not only in the United States—by second-rate physicists who, lacking sufficient ability, fail to qualify for key research positions in departments of physics or cosmology. This kind of natural selection is thus not determined exclusively by personal preferences. This is also why no philosopher will be able to secure a place for himself at the helm of science.

Yes, I do regard philosophical aesthetics as a collection of print not worth reading. At present there is no longer any difference between a work of art and a piece of garbage. Anyway, consent to obscenity and scatology is often a matter of chance. Connections—knowing the right person—turns art into a lottery of prominence, especially in the visual arts. One can curse this, but such an attitude no longer qualifies as philosophy—unless someone is willing to employ such condemnations as a rallying banner for our school of philosophers-aestheticians.

Leszek Kolakowski wrote once an article entitled "Ethics without a Statute" ("Etyka bez kodeksu"), exposing the ubiquitous internal contradictions in all ethical codes founded by various religious and secular systems. There can be no progress in the area where *no* commandments or other arbitrary dogmas are de facto observed. It is often argued that any ethical code, considered as a system of injunctions and prohibitions, always works in a society with a delay. How one might formalize or generalize such a theory of ethical delay—I have absolutely no idea. To me it is like trying to square the circle. There exist areas, like world politics, which are de facto excluded from ethics and, as the history of the United Nations exemplifies, there is no hope for any form of unification there.

Swirski: *In view of a progressive reconnecting of many scientific disciplines (biochemistry, psychophysics, econometrics, etc.), what hybrids do you foresee in the future? Can you comment on the viability and status of interdisciplinary research both in the sciences and humanities? In the age of progressive specialization, is it realistic to expect scholars to be conversant with multiple divergent disciplines?*

Lem: As for the reconnecting of academic disciplines, which are in the process of diverging, multiplying, sprouting increasing numbers of specialized branches on the tree of knowledge—I am a pessimist. The best evidence can be found, for example, in the high nonreductiveness (nonsimplifiability) of inquiry into broadly conceived bioprocesses (such as biogenesis, bioevolution, bioecology, etc.). No single and simple formalism could connect or reconnect the ever expanding Molochs of information yielded by research in these fields. Intensive computerization can slow down the pace of this outward radiation, but only at the cost of creating a paradox which I predicted thirty years ago in *Summa technologiae*. If computers indeed succeed in creating "knowledge concentrates" of colossal informational proportions, it is likely that these proportions will extend beyond the human potential for comprehension. Both we and our science will then find ourselves (as I described it in *Golem XIV*) under stewardship of a decidedly nonhuman type, cognitively "governed" by machines. This would be, in fact, a form of reconnection, but a very bitter one, since it would have been achieved beyond the threshold of the human ability for appreciation.

Today it is becoming increasingly clear that the machinery of life present in every cell, in every trajectory of the evolution of life on Earth, is much more complicated than first imagined after the discovery of the DNA code. It appears that man has been "built" by evolutionary anthropogenesis with methods that are both "inhuman" and "antihuman" to the highest degree— at least if we look upon our own creation from the point of view of engineering, this technologically developed prosthesis of the human mind. It is for this reason that difficulties multiply. Communication among differentiating and diversifying specialties will be increasingly inhibited. Even today, within mathematics, a topologist and an expert in number theory encounter very grave difficulties in communication. How to reverse this trend without transferring power to computers, I haven't the foggiest idea.

As far as the fate of literary studies is concerned, I fear that in the future it is going to play an ever more *marginal* role, and that all efforts to "catch up" with the sciences will turn out to be fruitless. Today we can best see this future in the example of poststructuralism and deconstruction—modern neoscholastics, empty and futile, especially when contrasted with the slow but incessant progress of the empirical disciplines, which continue to chip away at the linguistic edifice of human thought and language (e.g., through research in neurology and the study of the brain). In other words, with regard to the interdisciplinary future of literary versus empirical studies, I foresee regression. It is a little bit like science fiction: more and more fiction, and less and less science. This applies equally to scholars who try to make up for the "retardation" of their field, employing more and more labyrinthine systems of thought (reflected in their terminology). After all, structuralism was such an attempt to introduce sui generis reductionism into scholarship, but it only ended up throwing out the baby with the bath water.

Swirski: *Do you think that the work of Stephen Hawking on quantum radiation of black holes provides the much sought-after common framework for classical Einsteinian physics and quantum physics? Do you think that the paradigmatic position of the physical sciences is likely to be usurped in the twenty-first century? Can you think of a better test of a computer's "consciousness" than Alan Turing's operational one? In "The History of Bitic Literature" (from* Imaginary Magnitude) *you claim that a particular hardware configuration could be relevant to a given computer author's literary production; however, all Turing machines are supposed to be computationally equivalent, thus apparently undermining the distinction between different systems/hardwares.*

Lem: The work of Hawking is particularly precious since it is one of the first places where quantum mechanics meets Einstein's General Theory of Relativity. At the same time, I think that physics and biology will run neck and neck in the race for supremacy in the twenty-first century. The result of this competition will depend, however, not just on scientific progress itself, but even more on politicians and their investment policies. I fear, though, that politicians the world over are going to demonstrate an increasingly poor understanding of the significance of their "stewardship" of the sciences (notable even today in their attitude to basic research and development).

The next stage in computer evolution has to be parallel processing—what happens in our own brains. I am not familiar enough with the contemporary state of the theories that were introduced forty or fifty years ago, from John von Neumann and his contemporary "founding fathers" of cybernetics, to Claude Shannon, one of the first information scientists. Nevertheless I believe von Neumann was right to criticize the purely iterative, linear, combinatorial work of finite automata. It is true that they are the simplest to model mathematically, since all algorithmic, recurrent functions are amenable to easy formalization, but the chasm emerging from Gödel's work can be spanned only with the aid of the same kind of strategies that have been found by trial and error over the past four billion years by the "mathematically deficient" evolution. I am afraid we will never succeed in coming up with anything better: if something initiated four billion years ago "tried and erred" for four billion years, I find it hard to believe that we are likely to hit upon a royal "shortcut" to our needs and goals that has not been investigated by evolution.

In my previous writings I have on occasion expressed doubts as to whether Turing's test can be accepted as infallible. Today I doubt it more than ever. The result of the test depends on 1) the person conducting the test, 2) the program, and 3) the processing powers of the computer. People of not more than average intelligence have *already* been led astray by a properly written program.[8] As Nalimov—an expert in probability—already observed, it is the very nonalgorithmic nature of texts in all natural languages (and thus their translational nonidentity) that precludes anything but their "interpretation," that is, projection of one text into another. It is for this reason that it is impossible for a thousand translators to render the same Shakespearean play into German or Polish in the same way, to the letter. This goes to show that no algorithm—and by extension, no finite automata, which can *all* be emulated by the simplest Turing machine—could ever model the human brain. On the other hand, parallel processing allows just that, but all that is yet in the future. Today the field is dominated by primitive computational "strongmen," computers of the last generation—dinosaurs in whom reason will not flare up, just as it never did in the real dinosaurs in the past.

Swirski: *There is a vicious circle in the relation of mathematics to the human sciences (and literary scholarship). Since the latter are so far behind the physical sciences, few mathematicians of the highest caliber are attracted to forging mathematical tools which would be suitable for work in the humanities. This, of course, results in an even greater gap, which further diminishes the attractiveness of the field to potential contributors from mathematics. Would you care to comment on this state of affairs, and on the need for mathematizing the humanities in general, and literary studies in particular?*

Lem: The irreducibility of literary studies to mathematics cannot be overcome. Language is fundamentally nonmathematizable (in Hilbert's sense); it is simply impossible to circumvent the Gödelian collapse. Still, there is nothing to get upset about. *Every* work, not even necessarily a work of fiction, is interpretable by its readers in a number of ways, and nothing can reduce this state of affairs to uniqueness and unity (naturally, totalitarian dictatorships can enforce a certain orthodoxy of reading, but what does this have to do with truth?). In other words, I do not subscribe to the view that literary studies ought to be pressed into mathematization at all; this would be for it the bed of Procrustes.

On the other hand, it is possible to employ nondigital simulations and other techniques for our purposes, but the whole thing will always be overseen by people. Furthermore, there can always be a stupid mathematician and an astute scholar; also frequently idiots equipped with a considerable "force of entry" are able to achieve fame owing merely to the prevailing fashion, but what does such a state of affairs have to do with cognition? On top of everything, our approach to art in all of its manifestations cannot be restricted to the cognitive gain, that is, the increase in knowledge thus obtained, much as the meta-attitude to works of art (e.g., literary or aesthetic theory) cannot be restricted to a purely epistemic analysis and diagnosis. This is so because the highest court of appeal, as far as judgment and evaluation of artworks are concerned, rests neither with critics nor metacritics, but with the society which partakes in the reception of artistic productions.

In theory one could contemplate a situation where a totally secularized, infinitely permissive, consumptively gratified—in short, stable and materially affluent—society culls from all available artistic offerings only the greatest kitsch, the greatest sensation, the greatest pornography, the greatest trash. At the same time, buried somewhere in the catacombs of academe, persists a convent of savants who keep faith in a grand hierarchy of artworks now totally forgotten by the people at large. Such a situation is imaginable, but the whole exercise would seem pointless. Where religious convents are concerned, the picture is different: they derive their raison d'être from faith which, in such a case, is a sufficient argument for their existence. On the other hand, a convent of scholars, isolated from society, cannot even maintain that it painstakingly guards the highlights of some definite aesthetic and cognitive norms, since *there is nobody* for whom to preserve these treasures (unless it be the conviction that, like the prodigal son, future generations will some day return to the noble and difficult matters of art).

Let's look at it from another point of view. When "applied," theoretical physics can give results that may be both harmful (e.g., atomic energy) and useful (again atomic energy). However, theoretical physicists do not pursue their research in anticipation of gain, or out of servitude to the study of nature. On the contrary, they do not expect anything; their spontaneous activity, just like (supposedly) virtue, constitutes a reward in itself. On the other hand, scholars who study *Don Quixote* do not proceed to bury their work underground for centuries to come. Thus the fact that his work will circulate in a progressively more hermetic circle of scholars and critics *even today* has to be a sufficient reward for the literary scholar, because society at large obviously prefers *The Terminator* to Aristophanes or Joyce. For myself, the entire effort that I invested in the creation of an empirically based theory of literary works proved wasted. The compass needles of art and empirical science continue to point in different directions. It looks as if we must become reconciled to this state of affairs, because any convergence between them could be found only in some form of *sacrum* typical of religious faiths. The rest, as they say, is silence.

Literary theory has, of course, its own history. As I wrote in the introduction to *Philosophy of Chance,* trouble begins even with the very conception of a monolithic theory of literary works, which is either doomed to harmful simplifications or to the encroachment of arbitrariness. Why? Literary theory oversees a massive number of very different disciplines which, on top of everything, are all at different stages of development. To begin with, one may debate and inquire into an artwork's ontological status. The next set of dilemmas will be involved in the fact that the work is a species of linguistic creation (statement). Next in line are problems of counterfactuality (in primitive terms: literature lies since no Othello or Hamlet ever existed). These are primitive accusations, but not for a logician. Next we encounter questions about the work's systems of reference. In general, artworks refer to a multitude of such systems, in varying proportions: to the contemporary world as their *genius temporis,* to socio-political configurations, to genre paradigms of a given style, to a set of "virtual readers," perhaps even to the subset of the former comprised by reviewers and critics (for my part, I never paid any attention to this last subset, but my behavior is not typical of other writers). Other systems of reference: the canons of aesthetics of the language, and the dominant system of *savoir vivre* (even de Sade systematically employed periphrasis when describing the activities of coprophagists, sodomizers, etc., in deference to the spirit of the times). In most cases the number of such virtual, latent reference systems will form an infinite set, since one can always read a literary work by approaching it from a direction that is completely new in the context and the history of reception of the work. If one were to dream of designing a theory of interpretation applicable without exception to any and every literary work of the past, present, and future (just as Newton's theory is applicable to any system of gravitating bodies), it should by now be evident how fundamentally "undesignable" such a theory must be, having to face the specter of *regressus ad infinitum*.

There is a multitude of phenomena which we do not fully understand. An example: the works of Shakespeare do not age for the English-speaking parts of the world, which cannot be said for his translations into other languages, where new updated translations must always be made. Why is this so? Because there is no need to "ameliorate" Shakespeare himself (I am not speaking, of course, of bowdlerism). On the other hand, what does change are our ways of reception and interpretation. This is the reason why translations, those interpretive projections of Shakespeare's work (or at least its interpretable part) into a foreign language, are not exempt from aging. Interpretations have a limited time span even when their matrix—that is, the original work—is accepted as an immortal contribution to the literature of the era. The number of degrees of freedom in criticism and literary theory is not only incalculable a priori; there are other limitations as well, imposed by a separate group of factors. For example, we do not discredit works just because they do not depict acts of defecation or urination, even as they evidently strive for ultrarealism. One could, after all, take issue with such omissions, since depictions of the above mentioned type would be permissible in current idiom (having said that, I must add that there are obviously a number of contemporary works which obviously feast on everything that tastes of obscenity).

Finally, there are no other methods of qualifying a work's artistic excellence than "suasive": without the proverbial "eye of the beholder" the work cannot exist at all, which makes readers the most basic system of reference. It is for this reason that literary works sometimes die out even before their authors' passing, just because they are no longer read by anybody. Another distinctive quality of a work is its singularity, deserving to be described in terms of its "resistance" to the passing of time (the same quality that transforms most of yesterday's best-sellers into deadness incarnate). One could continue in this way, multiplying factors which codetermine and condition the reception of works of literature, reinforcing the conclusion that no mathematical theory can be of avail here. The same applies to information theory, which can only approach prose and poetry as different specimens of linguistic degeneracy.

Swirski: *Following von Neumann's breakthrough in game theory in the 1940s, and the rapid development of the field in the 1950s and 1960s (Nash equilibria, Prisoner's Dilemma), few significant mathematical tools seem to have been added to it since (with the exception, perhaps, of Harsanyi's theory of "types"). Could you comment on this apparent halt in the development of the field? What do you conceive to be its potential for application in literary studies? Could it be genre modeling, as in your study of de Sade? Or ordinal analysis of conflict situations described in literary texts? Or even pragmatic modeling of the game between the author and the reader? Is game theory particularly suited to lead interdisciplinary studies of literature?*

Lem: Game theory is still in its infancy, since it is as yet too primitive to be applied in such crucial areas as economics or politics with reasonable, *predictive* results. A fortiori, this critique applies equally to bio-evolution and techno-evolution. It is obvious today that Nicolas Rashewsky's efforts from fifty years ago to mathematize life processes were grossly premature, and the failure on the part of both biologists and mathematicians to recognize their respective ignorance preempted any effective research. In short, there is a lot of work waiting to be accomplished yet in the younger, less established disciplines. Newborns and infants are not immediately identifiable as future Nobel Prize winners, future geniuses, future inventors or discoverers; moreover, science has always progressed in leaps and bounds.

Success within literary theory can be only of local nature. By that token, a comprehensive grafting of one type of research onto a completely different domain, especially one involving art and artistic creations, is not a fully legitimate enterprise. My application of game theoretic concepts and terminology to de Sade was successful because his writings yield themselves quite well to this type of approach. Up until then, without exception, all Sadologists saw "the divine Marquis" not as an apologist of Evil in all its incarnations but as a "professor" of Sex, a kind of Beelzebub worth serving because it is (even in coprophagy) "very pleasant." For my part I tried to segregate sex from the doctrine in order to reveal its "infrastructure"—the ethic of Evil. This approach cannot succeed in every case: de Sade was, after all, a meagre *littérateur* but a deviant of immense proportions (Camus showed it well *suo tempori* in his introduction to de Sade's *Justine*).

Every literary work demands its own proper treatment whenever critical analysis comes into play. On top of this problem, there is always the overarching question of the currently dominant critical fashion. In my particular case, I could never have cared less for the reigning scholarly fads. I conduct my inquiries in the spirit of rationalism which is, unfortunately, quite inimical to the dictates of the current critical vogue. Still: where no single set of criteria is in place as to the choice of the "correct" critical method, one is free to do just as one pleases.

I feel the need to comment on the hopes expressed in your question about the chances of mathematizing literary theory, or even more generally, aesthetic theory. Dealing with questions of this kind, we must keep in mind that mathematics is devoid of semantic content only in its most extreme forms, for example, as a programming language for digital computers (understood at this point exclusively as finite automata). Mathematics is a language sui generis, and as such is no stranger to philosophical interpretation, at least in the ontological sense. One can, after all, ascribe different types of existence to mathematical formulae, from constructivism to Platonism, for example. Since any language can be abused as well as used, the introduction of mathematics to any area of knowledge is never a guarantee of improved results. Simply put, one can mathematize complete idiocies. The use of powerful mathematic tools is productive only inasmuch as it follows a previous introduction of an adequate methodological base.

An example from painting: abstract painting can be approached as a strongly degenerate form of language. This should not be taken as a disparaging or even evaluative comment: it is used here in the same sense in which one speaks in physics of, for example, degenerate electron gas. A sufficiently degenerate language becomes so polyvalent, so multi-interpretable, that it obstructs the emergence even of a consistent, related group (set) of readings (receptions). In contrast to abstractions, realistic or naturalistic painting does not act as a language. Instead it assumes the status of diverse forms of symbols and symbolic allusions to its para-iconic content, such as mythology or even folk and fairy tale, as in the case of Hieronymus Bosch (naturally, there can always emerge hybrids like Pieter Breughel the Elder). Consequently, a painting which "translates" some proverb into various groups of motionless people is both symbolic and nonsymbolic, because language (the language of the proverb) is a system of semantic *reference*. It is clear that, apart from aesthetic value, such a painting has a certain semantic value as well, established in relation to a certain definite meaning. This aspect is analyzable by aesthetic theories used in the fine arts. At the same time we must realize that any sufficiently complex system is—in view of the theorems of information science—divisible into multiple subsystems of many diverse kinds. Of course in this situation the choice between the idiographic or nomothetic method depends more and more on the critic and increasingly less on the picture itself. To put it bluntly: viewers perceive whatever they shape, interpret, and aesthetically evaluate for themselves. Today such evaluations are already arbitrarily erratic, thanks to postmodernism which obliterated the boundary between a work of art and a piece of garbage.

The same phenomenon of linguistic degeneracy can be observed in literature, for example in different types of collage (as in Thomas Pynchon's *Gravity's Rainbow*). I must reiterate that the polyvalence—the almost unbounded permissiveness—of interpretation is essentially of the same nature as that of Rorschach tests. The viewer sees whatever is prompted to him by his brain's associative effort (the results can also indicate the perceived aesthetic value of the Rorschach test). Through this we reach the conclusion that in literature readers read *both* what is in the work as well as whatever they read "into" it. As I have written in my *Philosophy of Chance,* there is no other cap on the activity of the reader other than the "stopping rules" of established canons of reception. The sociology of literature crosses paths here with group psychology, being these days a consequence of escalating commercial pressures combined with simple human inertia and stimulated even further by the invasion of visual media. No single theory alone could congruously integrate such a proliferation of heterogenous factors. In these circumstances any hopes for integrating the selective and creative powers of mathematics into aesthetics must be regarded as futile. The mainstream trends in the contemporary elite of the belles lettres seem to favor multifactorial phrase-stimuli, somewhat in the manner of poetry, where the creator's mind is free to become a mixer of meanings, thus edging even closer (and in an even more indefinable form) to the polyvalence of the Rorschach type. In cases like this, mathematics is rendered almost totally helpless.

We can see that only a certain subset of literary works yields itself in a promising way to game theoretic treatment. Only where the narrative clearly depicts conflict situations is one able to model plot-based games; *Hamlet,* for example, can be analyzed very well in game theoretic terms. The trouble is, however, that game theory does not have the power to detect and describe the work's axiological and aesthetic properties. Faced with these, game theory is perforce as neutral as the various types of literary structuralism previously had been.

Swirski: *In* Summa technologiae *you have discussed the prospects for biology and molecular/genetic research which, in view of the most recent achievements in these fields, seem quite prescient. What further developments (considered typologically) do you envisage in the biosciences?*

Lem: There is no doubt in my mind that the next century will be an era of biotechnology, but it would be impossible even to sketch the directions of this development. Biology will certainly give rise to biotechnology—this order of things corresponds to the spirit of our times. In the old days James Watt would first invent the steam engine, only later to be followed by various theoreticians who would mathematize the physical aspects of steam engines, bringing in the concepts of entropy and other laws of thermodynamics, adiabatic processes, and so on. These days things are different: it is theories which give rise to technological instrumental advances. Hypotheses point the way to falsifiable theories, and these in turn initiate concrete applications which subsequently can be utilized on an industrial scale. I suspect that this is also going to happen in our own case, meaning that we will witness an invasion of biotechnology into the human organism. The limiting case here is, of course, autoevolution, a possibility rife with extreme dangers in the case of our species. Most probably we will also witness a new phase in the battle against diseases and epidemics, forced on us by the necessity to take the pressure off the increasingly less efficacious antibiotics. Further still, future efforts will most likely be directed against the processes of aging and decay. I also anticipate the flourishing of genetic engineering, especially when used in combat with cancer and deficiencies in the genetic makeup of the human organism. Finally there are the already blooming fields—the industrialization of biotechnologically "piloted" pharmacology as well as the realm of mass food consumption (it all started with too quickly rotting tomatoes on a supermarket shelf).

Swirski: *Could you comment on the ever widening gap between ethical theory and practice and the relentless challenges to our "Victorian" mores posed daily by new bio- and computer technologies?*

Lem: The universal and still growing lag between present-day reality and all ethical codes, whether of the transcendental or secular humanist persuasion, is a result of a number of factors. To begin, the downfall of the Soviet Union deprived us of an enemy and put an end to the polarization of the world into black and white—the "evil empire and its acolytes" on the one hand and the "democratic forces" (the United States and Western Europe) on the other. Second: we have entered the epoch of excessive liberties. Through *horror vacui* we are being rapidly overrun by all varieties of nationalism and regionalism, leaving us in a mess which is highly conducive to conflicts among religious creeds as well as to political chaos. Economy remains impenetrable to physical or mathematical analysis and continues to act in an elemental fashion. Also the proliferation of information technologies has created a communications network spanning the entire globe: the world is short-circuited informationally, so that reverberations of events taking place in Japan or Algeria ricochet all the way to America. The roster of such phenomena is, of course, much more extensive. Moreover, the result of this hodgepodge of sundry factors assumes the forms of modern barbarism, atavism (soccer spectators painting their faces like Maori warriors), or deregulation, which extends even to the canons of *savoir vivre* (suffice it to compare the portrayal of men and women in Hollywood pictures sixty years ago and today).

The number of factors destabilizing the social homeostasis continues to grow. We are witness to a series of collapses, including the collapse of the accepted hierarchy of authority, with progressive secularization precipitating aggressive fundamentalist reactions in the centers of religious power (involving not only ayatollahs). Pathologies of escapism multiply: escape into narcotics, escape from the family, escape from any type of cultural taboo in the form of a "drive away from captivity"; we see signs of domination of the visual media over "Gutenberg's Galaxy," and so on. At the same time man with his intellectual capacities, his mental "condensity" and "reactiveness," is identical biologically to what he was 100,000 years ago. Civilization is simply drowning us all: we can no longer cope with it even at the threshold of the twenty-first century, while the demographic peril in the Third World is like a violent thunderstorm brewing just beyond the horizon. All this cannot but exert a paralyzing and anesthetizing effect on ethics, giving us as a result a new type of "man without conscience," capable of any crime because fed on images of crime all his life. Desperately looking in this turbulent sea for an Archimedean point of rest, people try to find it, for example, in sex or in various forms of pathology, *because a madman must above all be self-reliant, as long as his madness defines and orders his inner world.* To make a long story short: the traditionally inherited types of ethics are all rapidly becoming impotent.

Swirski: *How do you see your fictional and nonfictional work in relation to Polish science and philosophy? Have you ever enjoyed any meaningful contacts, mutual intellectual and theoretical stimulation, recognition and support (I am thinking, for example, of your cofounding of the Polish Cybernetic Society) from them? What is the status of Polish (or more generally, Slavic) science today? What are its prospects in the face of chronic underfunding?*

Lem: Luckily the answer to this question can be brief. In Poland there are no Lemologists; nobody betrays much interest in my own variety of philosophizing, including Polish scientists. The simplest way to give you an answer is as follows: if one takes my writings as a probe, or a kind of thermometer implanted in the society, then at once the situation becomes crystal clear. In Russia I've had editions of over seven million copies (of which over three million came out already after the fall of communism); in the united Germany my editions have also topped seven million; in Poland the printings of my books are in the range of only twenty-five to thirty-five thousand, and don't even include the nonfictional titles (my Polish editions before the fall of the communist government reached the total of 4.4 million).

One remark here: my alleged role in the creation of the Polish Cybernetic Society is a myth which I do not know to whom I should attribute, and which has been perpetuated by my foreign-language publishers. As a matter of fact I was only an ordinary member of the society and I hardly participated in its work in Poland. I got more involved in the Soviet Union in the 1960s, where I took part in the "rehabilitation" of cybernetics in the scientific circles. Although it is true that I continue to publish articles from the borderline of philosophy, information science, and theory of finite automata in *PC Magazine* (in Polish), this is a marginal activity, not involving any contacts with the sciences. While on that subject: Polish science is in a state of massive crisis since all the more talented minds emigrate to greener pastures. Things are somewhat different in Russia: there the resistance to the economic-political collapse is becoming much more pronounced. Russian science is certainly in considerable difficulties today, but slowly it begins to look like it might be turning the corner (astronautics is again playing the role of its draft horse). As for Polish science, the complete lack of understanding of the importance of financing scientific research bodes ill for the future.

Swirski: *In many of your works you reveal an intimate knowledge of "altered states"—hallucinations, drug-induced traumas, sensory deprivation, and the like. Is your knowledge secondhand (e.g., from scientific sources) or have you participated in some of these experiments? What are your present writing plans? Are any new translations of your works coming out?*

Lem: Yes, I have taken psilocybin under medical supervision. I had a chance to repeat this experiment, or at other times to take marijuana, but I didn't wish to. Evidently the normal state of my mind was sufficient for me. Hallucinogens help create a situation akin to a visual spectacle; following the experiment such estranged worlds did not exert any fascination for me.

I gave up writing fiction after 1988, following my return home to Poland from Austria. I still write articles from the domain of the philosophy of the future as well as other sundry essays; I am also in the process of preparing a collected edition of my works (since they are already available in Moscow and in Germany, it was hard not to consent to their publication in Poland). I should mention that clearly you find yourself in a much better position vis-à-vis my writings than anybody else who is forced to rely on translations. Yesterday I had a visit from a young lady who had tried to translate my *Summa technologiae* into English; for all the effort, she was forced to give up, even though she had had the help of an assistant who, apart from being fluent in both languages, was an information scientist by profession. In the Soviet Union *Summa* had been *suo tempore* translated by no less than seven people of different specialties, among them a physicist, an astrophysicist, a biologist, a mathematician, a Russian philologist, and a Slavonic language expert (in that case the costs of translation were not an issue since they were covered by the government). These days my U.S. publishers have great difficulties with finding translators.

Swirski: *Your own fiction is the best proof that literature can be a worthy cognitive device, but it would be interesting if you could comment on fictional*

modeling in relation to broad cognitive questions (validity, extent, truth, useful-
ness, etc.). How do you see general trends in the European and American literary
culture? Would you care to prognosticate its near and far future?

Lem: I have no doubts that, writing my books over the years, I have been swimming against the current of the prevalent fashion. It is enough to count the number of corpses (murders, killings) in my books and to juxtapose it with what constitutes the norm in contemporary fiction. One would look in vain in my works for deviants, sadists, madmen, sex maniacs, parricides, prostitutes, criminals, mafiosi, or drug dealers, which are the staple diet of the avalanche of print available in Poland and in the rest of the world. I swam against the current because I had always been fascinated with the human species (*Homo sapiens* as the last living type of hominids), while being perfectly indifferent to its individual variations. Today everything that I have done may be regarded as totally anachronistic, but I don't see how that can be helped. It is unfortunate that the printing numbers have already started to define a writer's rank. Maybe I exaggerate a bit in my diagnosis, but not too much. I would not dare prognosticate on the future of "Gutenberg's Galaxy" for fear that the twenty-first century, which I will not live long enough to see, has only a dismal fate for literature in its store.

Last but not least: I prefer to answer interdisciplinary inquiries from the borderline of philosophy of science and literature rather than get bogged down in questions concerning my own (science-)fictional works. The former approach is certainly more fruitful; as far as the latter is concerned, a writer should not critique his own writings, but leave it up to the critics.

Translated by Peter Swirski

Notes

1. Preformism is a biological theory according to which the individual, with all its parts, preexists in the embryo and grows from microscopic to normal proportions during embryogenesis, as opposed to epigenetic theory, according to which an embryo is formed by a series of new formations or successive differentiations. *Tertium datur* may be translated as "The middle cannot be excluded." Lem refers here to the principle of excluded middle—*tertium non datur.*

2. *Ignoramus et ignorabimus* translates as "we don't know and we won't know" or "we are ignorant and we will remain ignorant."

3. Engram is a term from psychology; it denotes the residual effect of an experience in memory.

4. Technobiocenosis here refers to the concept of autoevolution: changes in human hereditary makeup effected by technological means.

5. Oxford: Oxford University Press, 1989.

6. A Markov's chain is a type of stochastic process in which the future value of the variable depends only upon the present value and not on the sequence of past values.

7. Vasilii Nalimov, *Space, Time, and Life: The Probabilistic Pathways of Evolution* (Philadelphia: ISI Press, 1985).

8. See Joseph Weizenbaum, *Computer Power and Human Reason* (Harmondsworth, Middlesex: Penguin, 1984).

Stanislaw Lem: Bibliography

This bibliography preserves the original publishing chronology of Lem's works. As most of them are now available in English, I have listed English editions wherever applicable, followed [in square brackets] by an original Polish publication date. Works available only in Polish are followed by my own English translation of their titles.

Books

Człowiek z Marsa [*Man From Mars*]. Katowice: 1946 [published weekly in *Nowy Świat Przygód*].
Astronauci [*The Astronauts*]. Warsaw: Czytelnik, 1951.
Sezam i inne opowiadania [*Sesame and Other Stories*]. Warsaw: Iskry, 1954.
Hospital of the Transfiguration. Trans. William Brand. San Diego: Harcourt, 1988 [1955].
Obłok Magellana [*The Magellan Nebula*]. Kraków: Wydawnictwo Literackie, 1955.
Dialogi [*Dialogues*]. Kraków: Wydawnictwo Literackie, 1957.
The Star Diaries. Trans. Michael Kandel. New York: Avon, 1977 [1957; several later stories from this cycle appeared in English as *Memoirs of a Space Traveler*].
Inwazja z Aldebarana [*Invasion from Aldebaran*]. Kraków: Wydawnictwo Literackie, 1959.
Eden. Trans. Marc E. Heine. San Diego: Harcourt, 1989 [1959].
The Investigation. Trans. Adele Milch. New York: Avon, 1976 [1959].
Księga robotów [*The Book of Robots*]. Warsaw: Iskry, 1961.
Memoirs Found in a Bathtub. Trans. Michael Kandel and Christine Rose. New York: Avon, 1976 [1961].
Return from the Stars. Trans. Barbara Marszal and Frank Simpson. New York: Avon, 1982 [1961].
Solaris. Trans. Joanna Kilmartin and Steve Cox. New York: Berkley, 1971 [1961].
Wejście na orbitę [*Orbital Entry*]. Kraków: Wydawnictwo Literackie, 1962.
Noc księżycowa [*The Lunar Night*]. Kraków: Wydawnictwo Literackie, 1963.
The Invincible. Trans. Wendayne Ackerman. Harmondsworth, Middlesex: Penguin, 1976 [1964].
Summa technologiae. Kraków: Wydawnictwo Literackie, 1964.

Mortal Engines. Trans. Michael Kandel. New York: Avon, 1982 [1964].
The Cyberiad: Fables for the Cybernetic Age. Trans. Michael Kandel. New York: Avon, 1976 [1965].
Ratujmy kosmos i inne opowiadania [*Let's Save the Cosmos and Other Stories*]. Kraków: Wydawnictwo Literackie, 1966.
Highcastle: A Remembrance. Trans. Michael Kandel. San Diego: Harcourt, 1995 [1966].
Tales of Pirx the Pilot. Trans. Louis Iribarne. New York: Avon, 1981 [1959–68].
His Master's Voice. Trans. Michael Kandel. San Diego: Harcourt, 1983 [1968].
Filozofia przypadku: literatura w świetle empirii [*Philosophy of Chance: Literature in Light of Empiricism*]. Kraków: Wydawnictwo Literackie, 1968.
Opowiadania [*Tales*]. Kraków: Wydawnictwo Literackie, 1969.
Fantastyka i futurologia [*Science Fiction and Futurology*]. Kraków: Wydawnictwo Literackie, 1970.
The Futurological Congress. Trans. Michael Kandel. New York: Avon, 1976 [1971].
A Perfect Vacuum. Trans. Michael Kandel. San Diego: Harcourt, 1983 [1971].
Imaginary Magnitude. Trans. Marc E. Heine. San Diego: Harcourt, 1985 [1973].
Rozprawy i szkice [*Essays and Sketches*]. Kraków: Wydawnictwo Literackie, 1975.
The Chain of Chance. Trans. Louis Iribarne. San Diego: Harcourt, 1984 [1976].
Maska [*The Mask*]. Kraków: Wydawnictwo Literackie, 1976 [published in English as part of *Mortal Engines*].
Suplement [*Supplement*]. Kraków: Wydawnictwo Literackie, 1976.
Powtórka [*Repetition*]. Warsaw: Iskry, 1979.
Golem XIV. Kraków: Wydawnictwo Literackie, 1981 [published in English as part of *Imaginary Magnitude*].
Memoirs of a Space Traveler. Trans. Joel Stern and Maria Święcicka-Ziemianek. San Diego: Harcourt, 1983 [see *The Star Diaries*].
More Tales of Pirx the Pilot. Trans. Louis Iribarne, Magdalena Majcherczyk, and Michael Kandel. San Diego: Harcourt, 1983 [1965–83].
Wizja lokalna [*On Site Inspection*]. Kraków: Wydawnictwo Literackie, 1983.
Microworlds: Writings on Science Fiction and Fantasy. Ed. Franz Rottensteiner. San Diego: Harcourt, 1984.
Prowokacja [*Provocation*]. Kraków: Wydawnictwo Literackie, 1984.
One Human Minute. Trans. Catherine S. Leach. San Diego: Harcourt, 1986 [1984–86].
Peace on Earth. Trans. Elinor Ford with Michael Kandel. San Diego: Harcourt, 1994 [1987].
Ciemność i pleśń [*Darkness and Mildew*]. Kraków: Wydawnictwo Literackie, 1988.
Fiasco. Trans. Michael Kandel. San Diego: Harcourt, 1988 [1987].

Essays and Articles in English

"Promethean Fire." Trans. Yuri Sdobnikov. *Soviet Literature* 5 (1968): 166–70.

"Ten Commandments of Reading the Magazines." Trans. Franz Rottensteiner. *Science Fiction Commentary* 6 (1969): 26.

"Sex in SF." Trans. Franz Rottensteiner. *Science Fiction Commentary* 3 (1970): 2–10, 40–49.

"Poland: SF in the Linguistic Trap." Trans. Franz Rottensteiner. *Science Fiction Commentary* 9 (1970): 27–33.

"You Must Pay for Any Progress." Trans. Franz Rottensteiner. *Science Fiction Commentary* 12 (1970): 19–24.

"Letter." *Science Fiction Commentary* 14 (1970): 5.

"Unitas Oppositorum: The Prose of Jorge Luis Borges." *Science Fiction Commentary* 20 (1971): 33–38.

"Review: *Robbers of the Future* by Sakyo Komatsu." Trans. Franz Rottensteiner. *Science Fiction Commentary* 23 (1971): 17–18.

"Lost Opportunities." Trans. Franz Rottensteiner. *Science Fiction Commentary* 24 (1971): 17–24.

"Robots in Science Fiction." Trans. Franz Rottensteiner. In *Science Fiction: The Other Side of Realism*, ed. Thomas Clareson. Bowling Green, Ohio: Popular, 1971.

"Letter." *Science Fiction Commentary* 26 (1972): 28–30, 89–90.

"Letter." *Science Fiction Commentary* 29 (1972): 10–12.

"Culture and Futurology." *Polish Perspectives* 16 (1973): 30–38.

"On the Structural Analysis of Science Fiction." Trans. Franz Rottensteiner and Bruce R. Gillespie. *Science-Fiction Studies* 1 (1973): 26–33.

"Remarks Occasioned by Dr. Plank's Essay 'Quixote's Mills.'" *Science-Fiction Studies* 2 (1973): 78–83.

"Reflections for 1974." *Polish Perspectives* 17 (1974): 3–8.

"Todorov's Fantastic Theory of Literature." Trans. Robert Abernathy. *Science-Fiction Studies* 1 (1974): 227–37.

"The Time-Travel Story and Related Matters of S(cience) F(iction) Structuring." Trans. Thomas H. Hoisington and Darko Suvin. *Science-Fiction Studies* 1 (1974): 143–54.

"Letter." *Science Fiction Commentary* 41/42 (1975): 90–92.

"In Response." *Science-Fiction Studies* 2 (1975): 169–70.

"Letter." *Science Fiction Commentary* 44/45 (1975): 96–97.

"Philip K. Dick: A Visionary among the Charlatans." Trans. Robert Abernathy. *Science-Fiction Studies* 2 (1975): 54–67.

"SF: A Hopeless Case—with Exceptions." Trans. Werner Koopman. In *Philip K. Dick: Electric Shepherd*, ed. Bruce Gillespie. Melbourne: Norstrilia, 1975.

"Cosmology and Science Fiction." *Science-Fiction Studies* 4 (1977): 107–10.

"Looking Down on Science Fiction: A Novelist's Choice for the World's Worst Writing." *Science-Fiction Studies* 4 (1977): 126–27. Originally published in the *Frankfurter Allgemeine Zeitung*, February 22, 1975.

"In Response to Professor Benford." *Science-Fiction Studies* 5 (1978): 92–93.

"The Profession of Science Fiction: XV: Answers to a Questionnaire." Trans. Maxim and Dolores Jakubowski. *Foundation* 15 (1979): 41–50.

"Review of W. S. Bainbridge's *The Space Flight Revolution*." Trans. Franz Rottensteiner. *Science-Fiction Studies* 6 (1979): 221–22.

"Planetary Chauvinism: Speculation on the 'Others.'" Trans. Franz Rottensteiner. *Second Look* 1 (1979): 5–9.

"From Big Bang to Heat Death." Trans. Franz Rottensteiner. *Second Look* 2 (1980): 38–39.

"Letter." *Science Fiction Commentary* 60/61 (1980): 4.

"A Conversation with Stanislaw Lem." *Amazing* 27 (January 1981): 116–19.

"Metafantasia: The Possibilities of Science Fiction." Trans. Etelka de Laczay and Istvan Csicsery-Ronay, Jr. *Science-Fiction Studies* 8 (March 1981): 54–71.

"About the Strugatskys' *Roadside Picnic*." Trans. Elsa Schieder. *Science-Fiction Studies* 10 (November 1983): 317–32.

"Chance and Order." Trans. Franz Rottensteiner. *New Yorker*, January 30, 1984.

"Remarks Occasioned by Antoni Slonimski's *The Torpedo of Time*." Trans. Elizabeth Kwasniewski. *Science-Fiction Studies* 11 (1984): 233–43.

"Zulawski's Silver Globe." Trans. Elizabeth Kwasniewski. *Science-Fiction Studies* 12 (1985): 1–5.

"On Stapledon's *Last and First Men*." Trans. Istvan Csicsery-Ronay, Jr. *Science-Fiction Studies* 13 (November 1986): 272–91.

"On the Genesis of *Wizja Lokalna* (*Eyewitness Account*)." Trans. Franz Rottensteiner and Istvan Csicsery-Ronay, Jr. *Science-Fiction Studies* 13 (November 1986): 382–86.

"H. G. Wells's *The War of the Worlds*." Trans. John Coutouvidis. In *Science Fiction Roots and Branches: Contemporary Critical Approaches*, ed. Rhys Garnett and R. J. Ellis. New York: St. Martin's, 1990.

"Smart Robots." Trans. Peter Swirski. *Spectrum* (forthcoming).

Critical Sources on Lem (in English)

Anninski, L. A. "On Lem's *The High Castle*." Trans. Nadia Peterson. *Science-Fiction Studies* 13 (November 1986): 345–51.

Astle, Richard. "Lem's Misreading of Todorov." *Science-Fiction Studies* 2 (1975): 167–69.

Balcerzak, Ewa. *Lem*. Trans. Krystyna Cekalska. Warsaw: Author's Agency, 1973.

Balcerzan, Edward. "Language and Ethics in Solaris." Trans. Konrad Brodzinski. *Science-Fiction Studies* 2 (1975): 152–56.

Barnouw, Dagmar. "Science Fiction as a Model for Probabilistic Worlds: Stanislaw Lem's Fantastic Empiricism." *Science-Fiction Studies* 6 (1979): 153–63.

Benford, Gregory. "On Lem on Cosmology and SF." *Science-Fiction Studies* 4 (1977): 316–17.

————. "Aliens and Knowability: A Scientist's Perspective." In *Bridges to Science Fiction,* ed. George Slusser et al. Carbondale: Southern Illinois University Press, 1980.

Blish, James. "Review of *Solaris.*" *Magazine of Fantasy and Science Fiction* 40 (May 1971): 42–43.

Brewster, Anne. "An Interview with Stanislaw Lem." *Science Fiction: A Review of Speculative Literature* 4 (1982): 6–8.

Caldwell, Patrice. "Earth Mothers or Male Memories: Wilhelm, Lem, and Future Women." In *Women Worldwalkers: New Dimensions of Science Fiction and Fantasy,* ed. Jane B. Weedman. Lubbock: Texas Tech Press, 1985.

Carter, Steven R. "The Science Fiction Mystery Novels of Asimov, Bester and Lem: Fusions and Foundations." *Clues* 1 (1980): 109–15.

Cheever, Leonard A. "Epistemological Chagrin: The Literary and Philosophical Antecedents of Stanislaw Lem's Romantic Misanthrope." *Science-Fiction Studies* 21 (July 1994): 212–24.

Csicsery-Ronay, Istvan, Jr. "Kafka and Science Fiction." *Newsletter of the Kafka Society of America* 7 (June 1983): 5–14.

————. "The Book Is the Alien: On Certain and Uncertain Readings of Lem's *Solaris.*" *Science-Fiction Studies* 12 (1985): 6–21.

————. "Editorial Introduction." *Science-Fiction Studies* 13 (November 1986): 235–41.

————. "Twenty-Two Answers and Two Postscripts: An Interview with Stanislaw Lem." Trans. Marek Lugowski. *Science-Fiction Studies* 13 (November 1986): 242–60.

————. "Modeling the Chaosphere: Stanislaw Lem's Alien Communications." In *Chaos and Order: Complex Dynamics in Literature and Science,* ed. N. Katherine Hayles. Chicago: University of Chicago Press, 1991.

Dann, Jack, and Gregory Benford. "Two Statements in Support of Sargent and Zebrowski." *Science-Fiction Studies* 4 (1977): 137–38.

Davis, J. Madison. "Quirks, Quarks, and Fairy Tales." *Bloomsbury Review* 5 (1985): 19–20.

————. "'Today's Exception Becomes Tomorrow's Rule': Stanislaw Lem's *The Chain of Chance.*" *Publications of the Mississippi Philological Association.* Jackson, Miss., 1985.

————. "The Hydra of Science Fiction." *Bloomsbury Review* 7 (1987): 22, 30.

————. "The Quest for Art: Lem's Analysis of Borges." *Extrapolation* 29 (1988): 53–64.

————. *Stanislaw Lem.* Mercer Island, Wash.: Starmont, 1990.

Dick, Philip K., and Pamela Sargent. "The Lem Affair (Continued)." *Science-Fiction Studies* 5 (1978): 84.

Easterbrook, Neil. "The Sublime Simulacra: Repetition, Reversal, and Re-Covery in Lem's *Solaris.*" *Critique* 36 (Spring 1995): 177–94.

Engel, Peter. "An Interview with Stanislaw Lem." Trans. John Sigda. *The Missouri Review* 7 (1984): 218–37.

Everman, Welch D. "The Paper World: Science Fiction in the Postmodern Era." In *Postmodern Fiction: A Bio-Bibliographical Guide,* ed. Larry McCaffery. New York: Greenwood, 1986.

Farmer, Phillip Jose. "A Letter to Mr. Lem." *Science Fiction Commentary* 25 (1971): 19–26.

———. "Pornograms and Supercomputers." *New York Times Book Review* (September 2, 1984): 4.

Federman, Raymond. "An Interview with Stanislaw Lem." *Science-Fiction Studies* 29 (1983): 2–14.

Field, David. "Fluid Worlds: Lem's *Solaris* and Nabokov's *Ada*." *Science-Fiction Studies* 13 (November 1986): 329–44.

Fogel, Stanley. "*The Investigation*: Stanislaw Lem's Pynchonesque Novel." *Riverside Quarterly* 6 (1977): 286–89.

Foster, Thomas, and Luise H. Morton. "God or Game Players: The Cosmos, William Paley and Stanislaw Lem." *The Polish Review* 32 (1987): 203–9.

Geier, Manfred. "Stanislaw Lem's Fantastic Ocean: Toward a Semantic Interpretation of *Solaris*." Trans. Edith Welliver. *Science-Fiction Studies* 19 (July 1992): 192–218.

Gräfrath, Bernd. "Taking 'Science Fiction' Seriously: Stanislaw Lem's Philosophy of Technology." *Research in Philosophy and Technology* 15 (1995).

Grey, Paul. "Sci-Phi." *Time* (September 17, 1984): 87–90.

Guffey, George R. "The Unconscious, Fantasy, and Science Fiction: Transformations in Bradbury's *Martian Chronicles* and Lem's *Solaris*." In *Bridges to Fantasy,* ed. George E. Slusser et al. Carbondale: Southern Illinois University Press, 1982.

———. "Noise, Information, and Statistics in Stanislaw Lem's *The Investigation*." In *Hard Science Fiction,* ed. George E. Slusser and Eric S. Rabkin. Carbondale: Southern Illinois University Press, 1986.

Gunn, James. "On the Lem Affair." *Science-Fiction Studies* 4 (1977): 314–16.

Hayles, N. Katherine. "Space for Writing: Stanislaw Lem and the Dialectic 'That Guides My Pen.'" *Science-Fiction Studies* 13 (November 1986): 292–312.

———. "Chaos and Dialectic: Stanislaw Lem and the Space of Writing." *Chaos Bound: Orderly Disorder in Contemporary Literature and Science.* Ithaca, N.Y.: Cornell University Press, 1990.

Helford, Elyce Rae. "'We Are Only Seeking Man': Gender, Psychoanalysis, and Stanislaw Lem's *Solaris*." *Science-Fiction Studies* 19 (July 1992): 167–77.

Hofstadter, Douglas R., and Daniel C. Dennett. "Reflections." *The Mind's I: Fantasies and Reflections on Self and Soul.* New York: Basic, 1981.

Jarzebski, Jerzy. "Stanislaw Lem, Rationalist and Visionary." Trans. Franz Rottensteiner. *Science-Fiction Studies* 4 (1977): 110–25.

————. "Stanislaw Lem's *Star Diaries*." Trans. Franz Rottensteiner and Istvan Csicsery-Ronay, Jr. *Science-Fiction Studies* 13 (November 1986): 361–73.

————. "The World as Code and Labyrinth: Stanislaw Lem's *Memoirs Found in a Bathtub*." Trans. Franz Rottensteiner. In *Science Fiction Roots and Branches: Contemporary Critical Approaches,* ed. Rhys Garnett and R. J. Ellis. New York: St. Martin's, 1990.

Jonas, Gerald. "Looking for the Glitch." *New York Times Book Review* (February 17, 1980): 7, 33.

Kandel, Michael A. "Stanislaw Lem on Men and Robots." *Extrapolation* 14 (1972): 13–24.

————. "Lem in Review (June 2238)." *Science-Fiction Studies* 11 (1977): 65–68.

————. "A Portrait of the Artist as a Thing Antedeluvian." *The Cosmic Carnival of Stanislaw Lem.* New York: Continuum, 1981.

————. "Introduction" to *Mortal Engines* by Stanislaw Lem. Trans. Michael Kandel. New York: Avon, 1982.

————. "Two Meditations on Stanislaw Lem." *Science-Fiction Studies* 13 (November 1986): 374–81.

————. "On Translating the Grammatical Wit of S. Lem into English." Unpublished manuscript.

Ketterer, David. "*Solaris* and the Illegitimate Suns of Science Fiction." *Extrapolation* 14 (1972): 73–89.

Kratz, Dennis. "Heroism in Science Fiction: Two Opposing Views." *Riverside Quarterly* 30 (1988): 81–88.

Lavery, David L. " 'The Genius of the Sea': Wallace Stevens' 'The Idea of Order at Key West,' Stanislaw Lem's *Solaris,* and the Earth as a Muse." *Extrapolation* 21 (1980): 101–5.

Le Guin, Ursula K. "European SF: Rottensteiner's Anthology, and the Strugatskys, and Lem." *Science-Fiction Studies* 1 (1974): 181–85.

————. "Science Fiction and Mrs. Brown." In *Science Fiction at Large,* ed. Peter Nicholls. London: Gollancz, 1976.

————. "Concerning the 'Lem Affair.' " *Science-Fiction Studies* 4 (1977): 100.

Lewis, Tom. "Review of *The Star Diaries*." *World Literature Today* 51 (Summer 1977): 464–65.

Liro, Joseph. "On Computers, Translation, and Stanislaw Lem." *Computers & Translation* 2 (April/June 1987): 89–104.

Livingston, Paisley. "Science, Reason, and Society." *Literature and Rationality: Ideas of Agency in Theory and Fiction.* Cambridge: Cambridge University Press, 1991.

————. "From Virtual Reality to Phantomatics and Back." Unpublished manuscript.

Lyau, Bradford. "Knowing the Unknown: Heinlein, Lem, and the Future." In *Storm Warnings: Science Fiction Confronts the Future,* ed. George E. Slusser et al. Carbondale: Southern Illinois University Press, 1987.

Mabee, Barbara. "Astronauts, Angels, and Time Machines: The Fantastic in Recent

German Democratic Republic Literature." In *The Celebration of the Fantastic: Selected Papers from the Tenth Anniversary International Conference on the Fantastic in the Arts,* ed. Donald E. Morse et al. Westport, Conn.: Greenwood, 1992.

Malekin, Peter. "The Self, the Referent, and the Real in Science Fiction and the Fantastic: Lem, Pynchon, Kubin, and Delany." In *Contours of the Fantastic: Selected Essays from the Eighth International Conference on the Fantastic in the Arts,* ed. Michele K. Langford. New York: Greenwood, 1994.

Malmgren, Carl D. "Towards a Definition of Science Fantasy." *Science-Fiction Studies* 15 (November 1988): 259–81.

———. "Self and Other in SF: Alien Encounters." *Science-Fiction Studies* 20 (March 1993): 15–33.

Martin, George R. "Review of *Return from the Stars.*" *Book World* (June 22, 1980): 7.

Meesdom, Tony. "The Gods Must Be Crazy: On the Utility of Playful Chaos in the Universe of Stanislaw Lem." In *Just the Other Day: Essays on the Future of the Future,* ed. Luk de Vos. Antwerp: EXA, 1985.

Miller, Edmund. "Stanislaw Lem and John Dickson Carr: Critics of the Scientific World-View." *Armchair Detective* 14 (1981): 341–43.

Mullen, R. D. "I Could Not Love Thee Dear, So Much." *Science-Fiction Studies* 4 (1977): 143–44.

Murphy, Patrick D. "The Realities of Unreal Worlds: King's *The Dead Zone,* Schmidt's *Kensho,* and Lem's *Solaris.*" In *Spectrum of the Fantastic,* ed. Donald Palumbo. Westport, Conn.: Greenwood, 1988.

Oates, Joyce Carol. "Post-Borgesian." *New York Times Book Review* (February 11, 1979): 7, 40.

Occiogrosso, Frank. "Threats of Rationalism: John Fowles, Stanislaw Lem, and the Detective Story." *Armchair Detective* 13 (1980): 4–7.

Offutt, Andrew. "How It Happened: One Bad Decision Leading to Another." *Science-Fiction Studies* 4 (1977): 138–43.

Parker, Jo Alyson. "Gendering the Robot: Stanislaw Lem's 'The Mask.'" *Science-Fiction Studies* 19 (July 1992): 178–91.

Philmus, Robert M. "The Cybernetic Paradigms of Stanislaw Lem." In *Hard Science-Fiction,* ed. George E. Slusser and Eric Rabkin. Carbondale: Southern Illinois University Press, 1986.

———. "Futurological Congress as Metageneric Text." *Science-Fiction Studies* 13 (November 1986): 313–28.

Potts, Stephen W. "Fiction: *A Perfect Vacuum.*" *Science Fiction & Fantasy Book Review* 1 (1979): 60.

———. "Dialogues Concerning Human Understanding: Empirical Views of God from Locke to Lem." In *Bridges to Science Fiction,* ed. George E. Slusser et al. Carbondale: Southern Illinois University Press, 1980.

Purcell, Mark. "Lem in English and French. A Checklist." *Luna Monthly* (June 1972): 11.

————. "Tarkovsky's Film *Solaris* (1972): A Freudian Slip?" *Extrapolation* 19 (1978): 126–31.

Rodnianskaia, Irina. "Two Faces of Stanislaw Lem: On *His Master's Voice*." Trans. Nadia Peterson. *Science-Fiction Studies* 13 (November 1986): 352–60.

Rose, Mark. *Alien Encounters: Anatomy of Science Fiction.* Cambridge, Mass.: Harvard University Press, 1981.

————. "Filling the Void: Verne, Wells, and Lem." *Science-Fiction Studies* 8 (1981): 121–42.

Rothfork, John. "Cybernetics and a Humanistic Fiction: Stanislaw Lem's *The Cyberiad*." *Research Studies* 45 (1977): 123–33.

————. "Having Everything Is Having Nothing: Stanislaw Lem vs. Utilitarianism." *Southwest Review* 66 (1981): 293–306.

————. "The Ghost in the Machine: Stanislaw Lem's *Mortal Engines*." *Liberal and Fine Arts Review* 4 (1984): 1–18.

————. "*Memoirs Found in a Bathtub*: Stanislaw Lem's Critique of Cybernetics." *Mosaic* 17 (1984): 53–71.

Rottensteiner, Franz. "Stanislaw Lem: A Profile." *Luna Monthly* (December 1971): 6.

Sargent, Pamela. "A Suggestion." *Science-Fiction Studies* 5 (1978): 84.

Sargent, Pamela, and George Zebrowski. "How It Happened: A Chronology of the 'Lem Affair.'" *Science-Fiction Studies* 4 (1977): 129–37.

Say, Donald. "An Interview with Stanislaw Lem." *Science Fiction Review* 3 (1974): 4–15.

Scarborough, John. "Stanislaw Lem." In *Science Fiction Writers,* ed. E. F. Bleiler. New York: Charles Scribner's Sons, 1982.

Scholes, Robert. "Lem's Fantastic Attack on Todorov." *Science-Fiction Studies* 2 (1975): 166–67.

————. *Structural Fabulation: An Essay on Fiction of the Future.* Notre Dame, Ind.: Notre Dame University Press, 1975.

Scholes, Robert, and Eric S. Rabkin. *Science Fiction: History. Science. Vision.* London: Oxford, 1977.

Schwab, Gabriele. "Cyborgs and Cybernetic Intertexts: On Postmodern Phantasms of Body and Mind." In *Intertextuality and Contemporary American Fiction,* ed. Patrick O'Donnell and Robert Davis. Baltimore: Johns Hopkins University Press, 1989.

Science-Fiction Studies 40 (1986). Special Lem issue.

Science-Fiction Studies 57 (1992). Special Lem issue.

Simonetta, Salvestroni. "The Science-Fiction Films of Andrei Tarkovsky." Trans. Robert M. Philmus. *Science-Fiction Studies* 14 (1987): 294–306.

Sire, James W. "Truths Too Bitter for This World." *Christianity Today* 20 (1978): 34–37.

Slusser, George E. "Structures of Apprehension: Lem, Heinlein and the Strugatskys." *Science-Fiction Studies* 16 (March 1989): 1–37.

Solotaroff, Theodore. *New York Times Book Review* (September 29, 1976): 1.

———. "A History of Science Fiction and More." *New York Times Book Review* (August 29, 1979): 1, 14–18.

"Stanislaw Lem and the SFWA." *Science-Fiction Studies* 4 (1977): 126–44.

Steiner, T. R. "Stanislaw Lem's Detective Stories: A Genre Extended." *Modern Fiction Studies* 29 (1983): 451–62.

Suvin, Darko. "The Open-Ended Parables of Stanislaw Lem and *Solaris*." Afterword. *Solaris*. Trans. from French by Joanna Kilmartin and Steve Cox. New York: Walker, 1970.

———. "A First Comment on Ms. Le Guin's Note on the 'Lem Affair.'" *Science-Fiction Studies* 4 (1977): 100.

———. "What Lem Actually Wrote: A Philologico-Ideological Note." *Science-Fiction Studies* 5 (1978): 85–87.

———. "The Social Consciousness of Science Fiction: Anglophone, Russian, and Mitteleuropean." *Proceedings of the Seventh Congress of the International Association of Comparative Literature*, ed. M. Dimic. Stuttgart: Bieber, 1979.

———. "Three World Paradigms for SF: Asimov, Yefremov, Lem." *Pacific Quarterly* 4 (1979): 271–83.

Swirski, Peter. "A Literary Monument Revisited: Davis' *Stanislaw Lem* and Seven Polish Books on Lem." *Science-Fiction Studies* 58 (1992): 411–17.

———. "Playing a Game of Ontology: A Postmodern Reading of *The Futurological Congress*." *Extrapolation* 33 (1992): 32–41.

———. "Computhors and Biterature: Machine-Written Fiction?" *SubStance* 70 (1993): 81–90.

———. "Of Games with the Universe: Preconceptions of Science in Stanislaw Lem's *The Invincible*." *Contemporary Literature* 35 (1994): 324–42.

———. "Game Theory in the Third Pentagon: A Study in Strategy and Rationality." *Criticism* 38 (1996): 303–30.

———. "Between Literature and Science: Poe and Lem." Unpublished manuscript.

Szpakowska, Malgorzata. "A Writer in No-Man's-Land." *Polish Perspectives* 10 (1971): 29–37

Theall, Donald F. "On SF as Symbolic Communication." *Science-Fiction Studies* 7 (1980): 253, 256–61.

Thomsen, Christian W. "Robot Ethics and Robot Parody: Remarks on Isaac Asimov's *I, Robot* and Some Critical Essays and Short Stories by Stanislaw Lem." In *The Mechanical God: Machines in Science Fiction*, ed. Thomas P. Dunn et al. Westport, Conn.: Greenwood, 1982.

Tierney, John. "A Mundane Master of Cosmic Visions." *Discover* (December 1986): 55–66.

Tighe, Carl. "Kozmik Kommie Konflikts: Stanislaw Lem's *Solaris*: An Eastern Block Parable." In *Science Fiction, Social Conflict and War*, ed. Philip John Davies. Manchester: Manchester University Press, 1990.

Updike, John. "Lem and Pym." *New Yorker* (February 26, 1979): 115–21.

————. "Review of *Return from the Stars*." *New Yorker* (September 8, 1980): 106–11.

Vonnegut, Kurt. "Only Kidding, Folks?" *The Nation* (May 13, 1978): 575.

Weinstone, Ann. "Resisting Monsters: Notes on *Solaris*." *Science-Fiction Studies* 21 (July 1994): 173–90.

Weissert, Thomas P. "Stanislaw Lem and a Topology of Mind." *Science-Fiction Studies* 19 (July 1992): 161–66.

Wilson, Reuel K. "Stanislaw Lem's Fiction and the Comic Absurd." *World Literature Today* 51 (1977): 549–53.

Wood, Michael. "Review of *Mortal Engines*." *New York Review of Books* (May 12, 1977): 36–37.

Yossef, Abraham. "Understanding Lem: *Solaris* Revisited." *Foundation* 46 (1989): 51–58.

Ziegfeld, Richard E. *Stanislaw Lem*. New York: Ungar, 1985.

Ziembiecki, Andrzej. "'. . . Knowing Is the Hero Of My Books . . .'" *Polish Perspectives* 9 (1979): 64–69.

Zivkovic, Zoran. "The Future without a Future: An Interview with Stanislaw Lem." *Pacific Quarterly* 4 (1979): 255–59.